Cassy,

wildspirit you love so deeply,
you walk in the fathers gifts and
heart. For you I hear the word
Expansion! I see you looking out
over the horizons amazed at all
God has done for you in a short
amount of time. This is your
year, your season. Your ministry
is being birthed. Pappa says
my daughter I'm so proud of you.
You will see his hand move greatly
in and through you. I see
many gifts in all of your children
Everything is going to be birthed this

YEAR. ♡

love
you my
beautiful Friend
♡

Sharell
Barrera

♡

2

Take Back Your Land

Prophetic Insight on How to Obtain
All That Belongs to You

Sharell D. Barrera

ISBN-10: 1719184399
ISBN-13: 978-1719184397

For Worldwide Distribution, Printed in the U.S.A

Dedication

I want to make a special dedication to my Dad. He passed away while I was writing the fourth chapter. He raised me since I was four years old, was my biggest fan, and my greatest hero. Whopper, I thank God for a Dad like you. We may not have been blood, but you are still my Dad.

Table of Contents

Endorsement

Sharell Barrera has become someone that I look up to and admire for her radical love for Jesus and for people. She joined our online school of ministry this year and we all got to watch her blast off like rocket ship into her God given destiny and her identity! It was so beautiful seeing this! It was like uncorking a bottle of so much God goodness that couldn't be contained any longer!

Sharell is no normal person nor is she supposed to be! She is someone who was designed by God to be VERY Bright Bold and Full of His Outrageous Outflowing LOVE! You are special too! Everyone is created to be their own unique beautiful self and to SHINE Jesus Brightly and beautifully through their unique personality and their special giftings in Him!

I am very thankful Sharell has taken the time to write this incredible book to help liberate and empower others to take back their land too. This book will help many others to uncork the God given destinies in their own lives and step into a newer brighter destiny and adventure in God. YAY!

I am glad you are reading this wonderful book and have fun taking back your land! You and Jesus can do this!

Jason Chin
Author of Love Says Go
Founder of Love Says Go Academy - Online School of
Supernatural Ministry
www.lovesaysgo.com

Testimonials

"Take Back Your Land was so eye opening to me. I realized that I can have the victory, I can overcome any obstacles in my life just by changing my words."

"I started following Sharell's Facebook Live Videos after being invited by a friend. I received healing in my eyes after she called out a word of knowledge. I have followed her every move ever since. Thank you for sharing your testimony Sharell. I had walked away from ministry after so much loss in my life and you lit the fire under me again."

"My faith has already increased by reading how to cultivate my dreams. This is one of the biggest points I missed in my walk with God."

"The profound insight in this book opened my eyes to a new level of understanding!"

"I'm so grateful for the life you lead Sharell. The sacrifices you have made to pursue everything God has for you has greatly inspired me."

"I had given up on my dreams until I read this book and I did not realize that my faith had grown so dim. I'm starting to believe again. Thank you Sharell for your faithfulness, may God richly bless you."

"I have known Sharell all her life. I have watched her grow into the woman she is today. She has let every hard trial help her to grow in Christ. It hasn't been without hard times, but through everything, she has brought God all the glory."

"Sharell's testimony inspired me to get closer to God and work harder on myself."

"I honestly never thought God could turn all the hardships I've been through into something wonderful for his glory. This book opened my heart and eyes. These decrees are life changing! I have already experienced so much breakthrough."

"This book gave me hope for the future! The way Sharell let God turn everything around for her inspires me to live life to the fullest. Thank you so much for going after God with your entire being! I was greatly blessed by your story, please write more."

"Through Sharell's influence, I have been able to truly learn what it is to walk in prophetic gifting's. As a person who's had the gifts for a number of years but never truly understand them, meeting a person like Sharell is a bit of a divine appointment. Honestly, I had no idea who she was, but I felt in my heart that she was a prophetess. Actually, that was my first response to her. I asked her "prophetess?" to which she confirmed. I have known her a short time, but in that time through her example and most notably her testimony, I have discovered my calling. We share a similar past: drug addiction, marriage issues, self-loathing, etc. However, her energy and presence is one that makes you want to follow her lead. I can honestly say I have made a friend for life whose teachings and singing I look forward to daily. I often catch myself singing her trade mark song "I'm free to be me." -Nick

"The first time I heard Sharell speak, I thought she was an established public figure in Christ that I had just come across, because the Holy Spirit's presence was so strong in her. The words she spoke when she discussed her life's story were so similar to mine, even though her story is much different than mine. It broke me in a way I needed to be broken and God used that breaking to reveal more healing in my relationship with Him."

"Every Christian has a story and God wants those stories told to touch lives. Everyone needs to know there is more, always more, to your relationship with God through Jesus Christ, whether you have believed for decades or days. My walk had become a struggle that needed a word of encouragement. Sharell answered the call of the Lord to speak encouragement and touched my life for God."

"No matter where you are in your faith or unbelief, I believe you too can benefit from hearing Sharell's story of salvation and growing faith. Jesus is the way, the truth, and the life, and Sharell Barrera is a shining example of how He transforms lives."

-Michael Hilbert

Acknowledgements

I first and foremost want to thank Jesus Christ. I give all the glory and honor to my King, my friend, my help in time of need. He never let me down and He never will. He has been my lawyer, my defender, my healer, my best friend. When I had not a soul to count on, He was there.

I also want to thank my husband, Melvin Barrera, for helping me believe in myself when nobody else did. He has helped me become the woman of God I am today.

My children, Kylene, Samuel, David, Trinity and Taylyn. You guys have loved me through everything. God`s power in you inspires me every day. I can't wait to see your destinies unfold.

Samuel, my son, you will change the World with your passion. You will be one of the greatest prophets of your time, as was prophesied over you before you were even born.

My dad, whom I lost while writing the fourth chapter of this book. This is for you.

Mom, you have always been there. You and Whopper are my number 1 fans! You never gave up on me.

Tawnia, you have always stood by my side since earliest childhood. I thank God for a sister I can always count on! We made it out.

Melissa, you have always encouraged me and been the sister I needed!

Kassie Courtney, Mariah Toney, Andrea Alesha, all of the Glover Family, and Michelle Jean, all are my sent family from God.

Yuli, my sister sent from God, your fire and your passion will change the world.

Nelson, you helped me see the truth! You're a true hero.

Sherri, my powerhouse sister! You're going to sell many music albums!

Davina, this is your year! Your character is one in a million.

Dana and Rigo, you will travel oversees in ministry,
Cadeshia your prayers are powerful! I can't wait to read your book!

Michelle, your love for Jesus will inspire the world.

Dawn Liniger, a true friend.

Ty and Amanda, you two became family.

Cassy Hupp, my school of ministry buddy.

Pastor Jerry and Shirley Thomas, you both changed my life forever.

Thanks to my faithful armor bearers, Amber Sanders, Michael Hilbert, Lee Baylis, and Yuli Leiva.

A huge special thanks to my teacher in school of supernatural, Love Says Go Academy, Jason Chin, your passion for people to experience Jesus has changed the World!

A special thank you to my copy editor, Lisa Henkes.

Darren Canning Ministries, you prophesied life and fire over my ministry and everything God was birthing in me. Thank you so much for imparting the fire which set me ablaze!

William Pollock Ministries, thank you for your help, encouragement, prayer covering, and for also lighting a fire under me.

I want to especially thank all of my family and friends who came into my life and urged me to go after God with everything in me. I would not be who I am today without you.

Chapter 1

Find Your Worth Before the World Does

A Word for You

Psalms 92:12 The Righteous Will flourish like a palm tree; they will grow like a cedar of Lebanon. Planted in the house of the Lord, they will flourish in the courts of our God. They will still bear fruit in old age; they will stay fresh and green, proclaiming 'the word of the Lord is upright; He is my rock, there is no wickedness in Him."

17

My Precious Child,

I have adorned you with my most precious gifts.

I'm well pleased with your heart continuing to bear fruit.

Not one Word I have spoken over you will return to me void.

I'm not finished with you yet. I will continue working out my goodness in you until My day of completion.

You are anointed, called, favored and blessed.

Look ahead towards your victory like David did with Goliath: he didn't look to the left or to the right. He didn't look at what he didn't have or to his past. He just moved ahead to claim his blessings.

I'm pouring new blessings, new oil, and new revelations. All you have to do is reach up and take it by faith.

I'm your strength.

I'm made perfect through your weakness.

Take heart my child, I will never leave you to do this on your own.

My love for you is like a burning flame.

The more you seek me the more you will find me. What I have for you is hidden in the secret place.

This is your year, your time, and your season.

My eyes are on the faithful.

You are like a tree planted near flowing streams of my blessings, you will flourish and grow in the time I have appointed for you.

I take delight in you my chosen.

Your heart has come a long way.

I have called you up and out to proclaim my word to the people of the Nations. You will go where I send you.

You have been faithful with little so I will bless you with much.

Get ready to take Back your Land.

There was a time it was very hard for me to think back to my childhood, just a lonely girl always crying out for attention. I would do anything to be noticed, even if it brought me physical harm. That unfortunately stayed with me for many years until just recently.

I experienced extreme freedom when I did 'the Daniel Fast' with my church. Since then, I started having visions of Jesus! During 'soaking' time (lingering in His presence), bits of memory would come. He has shown me short snapshots of my past which I had blocked from my mind.

On one such occasion, while folding laundry, I touched my nose to a freshly dried towel, loving the clean scent and as I breathed it in, I said, *"Jesus I wonder what it would be like to smell your fragrance."*

A memory suddenly flashed through my mind of when I was maybe eight. My Mom used to have a candy tin with roses on it, which I would obsessively breathe in. I couldn't get enough of breathing in the aroma. At once, I understood that it was the same scent Jesus carries, and I heard Him say, *"You now already know."*

Then my memory shot to my child self, surrounded by angels. I used to be able to see them, until the enemy brought attacks of fear and horribly painful experiences into my life. I lost the ability to see beautiful things in the spirit, and instead was tormented by seeing demonic things. It brought so much trauma and heartache. The enemy tried to pervert my God-given vision so that I could not see what God was doing anymore.

As a four-year-old child, I would crawl up in my infant brother's crib so I wouldn't be alone at night. I still remember the only way I could fall asleep was to smell the baby lotion on the top of his head, or hold onto my mother's cheek for comfort.

A family member living in the same house with us had been practicing witchcraft. They would duct tape me to chairs, duct tape my mouth shut, and leave me alone for hours, until I would pass out. All I had was God. I have always known He was there. The enemy tried to silence me from birth. The day I was born dead and was not supposed to be here, He intervened in my life.

When I was four, my parents divorced. All I knew was that my Dad was gone, though I barely knew him. He was too busy pursuing his dreams and not interested in his family. So, I found myself in a new family, with a man I hated because he stole my mom away. I looked him in the eyes at four years old and said, *"I will kill you!"* (He always teased me about it years later). In my world, he stole my mom and her all her attention, so I was always angry. All of these things I went through led me to be a child who was completely out of control, on at least six different medications. No one knew why I was acting up, including me. I had blocked out everything.

I grew up thinking and believing something was wrong with me, because that's what I was told. I took myself off all psychiatric medications, even though I was told it could kill me after a near overdose. As I grew of course I started self-medicating. I figured *'hey, I can fit in with people who actually think I'm funny and I can stay numb all the time!'* I thought I would never have to deal with my problems. I'd just block out the sexual perversion, the abuse, and all the trauma.

In the summers my brother and I were sent to my Dads, a man who never knew how to be a father because he never had parents. He was raised by babysitters while his parents pursued their dreams. He did his best and we always had a fun time, until my brother and I were left with drug-addicted babysitters that would physically harm us and abuse us. A lot of it I blocked out but there was one instance I will never forget: my brother was around three and I was six. We were eating dinner when my little brother grabbed a fork and our babysitter got angry because he was holding the fork the wrong way, so she stabbed him in the hand with her fork and drew blood. I remember the sudden surge of adrenaline and freaking out. I tried to run to the phone to call for help but she locked us in a room. We hid under the bed as she screamed and threw things at us. We screamed and cried until we were exhausted and fell asleep.

Never having known what a healthy family looked like, I just kept attracting one abusive person after another. That's what I thought I deserved.

It wasn't until this year I finally heard God say *"Why do you keep settling?"* What a wakeup call! I honestly didn't realize I have always surrounded myself with people who would bring me down, compete with me, make me feel unworthy, make me feel worthless with the exception of a wonderful husband, amazing children, and also my mother and stepdad. Even with my extended family, it has been a long and hard work in progress. It's easy to look on the outside of people and think *'they have it all together.'* But the struggle is real, the fight for peace and love in the home is real and it takes work, especially when all you have ever known is dysfunction.

There have been times I would cry out to God and say, *"I will never be good enough for anyone."* His reply was, *"Good, that's where I want you because you're good enough for me."* I guess I gave Him plenty to work with!

The saying 'you're most like the five people you surround yourself with' is true. I realized I couldn't be the one to always pull everyone up anymore. I had nothing left to give. It's so important to surround yourself with friends who lift you up as well.

If you don't know your own worth, then the world will tell you who you are. After a while, you will believe it. I realized that I couldn't minister to everyone who messages, calls, or comes over and if you want a healthy mind, neither can you. It's not that we aren't walking in love. But to keep moving forward, the first person we need to work on is ourselves. I can't tell you the importance of this. When you finally experience true freedom, you want healthy relationships. You desire good, honest people of good character to be around you. You deserve it!

This scripture has always come to my mind whenever I find myself being distracted by other people:

"Why do you look at the speck of sawdust in your brother's eye and pay no attention to the plank in your own eye?" Matthew 7:3

Jesus said this for a reason! If you only get one thing out of this book, I pray this is it! In order to have a healthy, functional life full of joy and peace, the number one person we all need to work on is ourselves. One time, as I sat and worried about someone I loved dearly who was needing to 'get their life together'- I heard the Holy Spirit say, *"This person will only get as much deliverance as you're willing to share."* I thought, *'Why do I need to always be the one?'* But we are called to live by example. We are called to love. A servant is never better than his master. We are all called to serve.

Your Gifts Are Not Your Identity

Don't mistake your gifts with your *identity*. This is something so many of us Christians do. I have been saved and off drugs and delivered for fifteen years now. But the enemy had woven a web around me. I thought that my many gifts, talents and abilities were what made me so awesome. So when other people didn't recognize this about me, I would question if they truly heard from the Lord. Wow! I have been judged so often by people that I refused to look at inwardly, I refused to see I was searching for acceptance through the things I could do, like sing and write music, prophesy, receive words of knowledge, and heal the sick. Was I thinking wrong? Yes.

The Daniel Fast was a huge turning point for me! I truly didn't realize I had come to a place where I cared so much about what other people thought of me. It had started to stifle out the voice of God!

The only approval we should seek is *His*.

"For anyone who exalts himself will be humbled, and he who humbles himself will be exalted." Mathew 23:12

Our ultimate goal should be seeking the Father for His approval, for His guidance, His leading. When we put *Him* first, everything else follows. We don't even have to search for our gifts, our gifts seek us out. When Jesus is the first and main focus, everything else flows into place. I have had to distance myself from all distractions, everything pulling at me in order to get these revelations. These are not things I learned from pastors or other people. This is me searching out the heart of God for my life.

We all have secrets, problems and hidden things to work on. Not one of us is perfect! You show me a perfect person who has it all together and I'll show you a person who's really good at faking it. The heart of God is for us to reach the destiny and plans he has set forth for us. I got tired of missing it. I knew there had to be a greater revelation, I knew there had to be more. I knew that He had a purpose for me. In discovering my identity, I had to pull away from everyone I knew, everyone that was familiar to me, especially people who would bring up my past or could never see the work that God was doing in me now. They were not worth risking my future.

Sometimes We Must Love from a Distance

If your future is truly important to you, if you truly desire to be everything God has called you to be, you will seek what He has for you in such a way that He's the only one that matters.

One of my favorite pastors, Greg Hess, once said, *"Sometimes you may be thinking you're always doing the right thing by spending time pouring into every single person you meet, but is it really what God has called you to do, just because it's good?"*

That has stuck with me for the past two years. I always thought doing the nice thing was what God wanted me to do. It wasn't until I really went after the heart of God that I realized not everything we think we are doing for the kingdom is what He's called us to do. There's many instances I can think of where God warned me or gave me internal 'checks' about certain people, but I refused to listen because I was still that little girl needing attention, even if I had to pay a price. I thought that I only wanted to see the best in everyone, and I kept putting my heart out there to get hurt some more.

1 Samuel 15:22 says "To obey is better than sacrifice..." As much as I loved people and wanted everyone to love me because of all the rejection I had faced, I was only setting myself up for more pain and rejection. I somehow attracted every single person like that. I remember years ago a friend tried to show me Proverbs 4:23, *"Above all else guard your heart, for everything you do flows from it."* But I just didn't get it. I kept giving so much of myself to others that it began to affect my family and my children in a negative way.

"If anyone does not know how to manage his own family, how can he take care of God's church?" 1 Timothy 3:5

Our families, children, and spouses must come first before ministering to anyone else. For some people, we are asked by Papa God to plant seeds and move on. This includes letting Jesus minister to us as well.

Since studying this year in the school of supernatural ministry (LSGA) with Jason Chin, we are learning how to get accurate prophetic words for people. So I went to my room, started praying for people, and I started asking Holy spirit about them when I heard Him say, *"It's your husband and your daughter who need prayer for back pain right now. Your family is your first ministry. They must come first."* Sure enough, I heard Holy Spirit correctly! They both needed love and prayer for back pain, just as He had said. Everyone else must come after. Everyone else needs to be loved from a distance, especially people who cause heartache, pain, drama, or chaos in your life. Their behavior doesn't warrant all of your attention. You are wasting precious moments of your God-given short life. When you waste it on people who refuse to see who you really are, you give away a special part of yourself. They need to be put on a shelf, so to speak, and of course prayed for and then left there. Let God deal with them.

"Do not take revenge, my dear friends, but leave room for God's wrath, for it is written, 'It is mine to avenge, I will repay' says the Lord." Romans 12:19

There have been so many situations I have been in where people did the most horrible things you could imagine to me. But when I truly gave it to God and never said a word, He was faithful to deal with them. I'll give you this example: there was one instance I took it into my own hands and then I asked God why He wasn't sticking up for me. I heard Him say, *"You already took it into your own hands."* I missed a great opportunity for God Himself, the 'Creator of all things'- to stick up for me! That was devastating for me! Trust me, it's much better to let God handle it for us than to seek revenge. Even more than that, get to a much better place where we don't even *want* revenge. We just want those people who hurt us to truly know Jesus. In all honesty, if they truly knew Him, they wouldn't be lashing out at us anyway. I've heard it said, *"Hurting people hurt people."* The bible says to 'bless your enemies'- but I can't think of many instances where I have seen people practice this.

I got saved after being a drug addict from the age of twelve, and then a good man finally came into my life. I had given up on love. I had gone through so much with men. My ex had tried to kill me. He would beat me, hold me down and torture me, pound on my chest, and would verbally abuse me for four straight years. It wasn't until he tried to choke me to death in front of our six-month-old that I got on my knees and cried out for God to save me.

I thought every man was abusive. When my husband came along, I fell in love at first glance, but figured he would be just like every other man that I had been with. Thank God, he never gave up on me! When he would say nice things, I would ask, *"Why aren't you being mean to me? Why don't you fight and argue with me?"* That's how used to abuse I was. You can't tell me it's easy to get out of that mind set when that's all you have ever known. My prince finally won my heart.

We ran off to Reno, Nevada to get married. My mom took me downstairs in our hotel to get my hair and make-up done. I overheard a lady in front of me talking about how she was getting married for the fourth time, and I started snickering and laughing and making jokes about her. I know she heard me. I saw the look on her face. I was still so filled with hurt and hatred from everything I went through. No excuses, I was just mean.

But something happened that started to change my life that day. That woman walked up and paid for my hair and makeup. Talk about heart break! Tears instantly started to fall as I suddenly realized how horrible I had been to her. The next day

I woke up with such a conviction from the Holy Spirit, all I wanted to do was find that lady and apologize. But I never found her. I truly believe God uses people to test our hearts here on earth at times.

"Do not forget to show hospitality to strangers, for by doing so some people have shown hospitality to angels without realizing it." Hebrews 13:2

His Love

I will never forget the day my husband and I walked into a little church in northern California. As I looked up from the pew, for the first time ever - I experienced the true love of Christ through the eyes of Pastor Jerry Thomas who illuminated the love of God! I could feel the tangible love of the Father in every word he spoke! It was like every word he said was for me, straight from God!

My husband and I both began to tremble and cry. God was delivering us exclusively by His love! No one was talking about drugs or how we needed to change our lives.

"It is the kindness of God that leads us to repentance." Romans 2:4

No one there knew who we were. My husband was one of the biggest meth dealers in northern California, and I was the biggest meth head. At that time, my daughter was being raised by her grandparents.

But the love I felt pierced my heart in such a way I had never felt before, at least not that I could remember. I still get emotional to this day thinking of how we ended up in that church.

My husband didn't want anything to do with God and I thought Christians were total fakes, so I didn't need what they were giving. I figured I knew God, and He was already always there for me. I never wanted to be like the people in the church I saw growing up.

I think we cried the entire service, it was unreal! Pastor Jerry was simply sharing the love of God, and it transformed our lives forever. It has been such an adventure ever since, all because of one man's faithfulness and love for Jesus! I will never forget walking out of church that day: I could see color in the sky for the first time! It was like I had been under a dark cloud for so long that it was like seeing for the first time! I had never noticed so many beautiful colors! I remember saying to my husband, "Look at the sky! Look at the colors! Isn't it beautiful?" He agreed like we were both experiencing the same thing.

We had no desire to smoke anymore, we threw our cigarettes out the window as we drove away from church that day! We have not looked back since, but it has been a crazy, awesome ride.

After we really started turning our lives around, all hell broke loose. It seemed to us like all the demons in hell came after us, especially me. I was almost killed several times and have been in several accidents, but God supernaturally saved me every time. I have also had several illnesses try to come at me, including a brain tumor.

I have not met anyone who's had the same experiences as I have. So when people judge me, or want the anointing on my life, they have no idea what I have had to walk through to get to where I am today. I wouldn't wish what I have gone through on my worst enemy. I'm not sharing my story to be pitied, or to say I had the worst life in the world. I share it with the hope of helping others who are struggling.

There is hope for you! God can take all the broken pieces and make something beautiful out of us, if we let Him.

When you realize how much Papa loves you, when you understand His heart beats for you, that He's cheering you on, He's celebrating every step you take, He leaves the ninety-nine to go after the one, then you will *know* He wants you to be happy. He wants you to see your worth so you can understand you have His abundant love. He says that you deserve to be celebrated, loved, honored and cared for. His love is like a never-ending waterfall. He's not distant. He's just waiting on you to come discover who He is. If you don't know Him yet, make it your most important prayer. Make it your biggest declaration. Make it your biggest dream. He must come first before anything else.

Get so full of God that He overflows to all of those around you. Holy Spirit can become your best friend. He tells secrets to His friends. He tells His friends special things which are to come.

Chapter 2

We All Have A Calling

A Word for You

Genesis 12:2 "I will make you into a great nation. I will bless you and make you famous, and you will be a blessing to others."

My Child,

I have placed great destiny and purpose in you. Nothing can stop my plans for your life.

You have seen Me work many miracles.

I will go before you in everything you do.

This is the time you lean on me, not your own understanding.

I will turn hearts towards you, for I am the God of man's own heart.

Dream BIG! I have placed those dreams in you. I planted the seeds, now it's up to you to water them.

I will give you all the desires of your heart, making all your plans succeed.

I know your heart is for My people, so My heart is for you.

I remain faithful to My words even when My people go astray.

I will continue to refine you and lead you into your destiny.

I'm sending the rain, the abundant showers of blessings.

I'm restoring everything to you. When I restore a thing, it's always better than before.

You will shine with My presence and glory.

Remain strong, grounded in My love.

The wicked will continue in their ways, but the righteous incline to My voice.

You are righteous. You are blessed. You hear My words, you have been faithful. I delight in your heart and your willingness to obey.

Today, I clothe you with a fresh anointing, a mantle of pureness, holiness and righteousness. You will shine like the stars for all to see as you step out in courage to silence the enemy.

Dwell under My wings, in My shadow. I will give you rest My child. For nothing can defeat you when I am with you. Nothing can separate you from My love. You are precious to Me, one of My favorites.

When you lift up your praise, I am there in the midst.

I'm sending you out, raising you up to be like a trumpet to the nations! When you open your mouth, I will give you the words to say.

I lift the humble in heart. I raise the lowly and the broken.

Have you ever struggled with your purpose or destiny? Have you ever just longed for words from a prophet or a great man or woman of God just to tell you everything you're supposed to be doing here on earth? I think we've all been there. I know I have.

Maybe you're like me: ever since I could walk and talk, I remember singing and knowing that's what my God-given gift and purpose was to do when I grew up. Maybe you're like many others who never had a passion, but you have been given several prophetic words of what your purpose is here on earth.

Receiving prophetic words are fantastic, but not as important as finding God's heart for your life. I can't tell you how many years I wasted chasing my passions and dreams, believing they were God's plans for me.

At some point in my Christian growth, I learned the power of *declaring God's Word and purposes*. My kids and I started every day declaring that I would be recording in Nashville and have songs on the radio. Within no time, I was contacted by talent scouts in Nashville, and began recording in a studio with famous people and got signed to a small country label!

Ultimately, none of it worked the way I thought it would. I had the *dream* correct, but the *purpose* wasn't there yet. I had not yet grown enough to understand that I needed to be *God-centered* to walk in the confidence of knowing who I am and what my purpose is *in HIM*.

So every person who came along and made me promises, I fell for it. I started to rely again on man and everything fell apart for me. I had what seemed like a great opportunity come to me, but I knew deep down that it wasn't an offer sanctioned by God. I was also taken advantage of by so many people because I trusted every person who said they were for me.

Many years ago while I still lived in Texas, I was given a prophetic word about my music by a dearly beloved man of God named Ferris Whitehead: "You will have many offers, but make sure you go with the right one."

Even though I had started to really get off the path, His word was still rooted in my heart. When an opportunity came from a country music legend, one established in the Hall of Fame, I was given a choice to pretty much sell off my identity and what I believed in. I couldn't do it, I refused. I knew deep down that choosing to stand on my principles, God would bless it. When my music was stolen, I let it go, and 'let God'.

I can only imagine if I would have sold out my life for a life of fame, what I would have become. I'm so thankful God empowered me to make a different choice. Even though I love country music, my passion is gospel which comes out of me naturally.

Though I have had many passions, dreams, and visions, Proverbs 3:6 motivates me:

"In everything you do, put God first, and he will direct you and crown your efforts with success."

It's easy and too often that we take our focus off Jesus and on to our own dreams and visions when really, it's about God's dreams and visions for us.

So how do we find His dreams for us? Only by seeking His heart for our lives. So often we think and say we want an encounter with God, but don't want to give God even ten minutes of the day! The only way to truly know God's heart-dream is to seek Him with all of our heart. When we ask and seek, He shows up!

Character Must Be Built to Hold the Dream

During the first few days of The Daniel Fast with my church, I would wake up and hear a couple of words from The Holy Spirit! Those words caused complete breakthrough for me! He would give me some small bits to make me eager to dig for more.

The first day of the Fast, I had a dream that I was entering into marriages with false gods. I woke up feeling disgusted and asked Holy Spirit why I had the dream. I heard Him say that I give way too much of my time and focus to social media, and other things which were wasting my time.

That was such a wakeup call for me! How can I know Jesus and His plans if I'm too busy for Him? I had to distance myself from many activities, and even some people in order to hear Him again. Honestly, in the past five years it has been a real struggle to hear His voice. I discovered that after I had walked through some serious trials, my heart had become hardened.

A dear friend of mine gave me a devotional by Joyce Meyer, and the first thing I read was someone telling her they couldn't hear God anymore! Joyce told the person to go back to the last time and ask forgiveness for not listening.

Yes, I had to go back and get right with God. I had allowed bitterness and anger into my heart. Sadly, the only person that hurt was me.

Proverbs 14:30 "A peaceful heart leads to a healthy body, but jealousy is like cancer to the bones." (NLT)

NIV says it this way: *"A heart at peace gives life to the body but envy rots the bones."*

I can honestly tell you I had arthritis pain from allowing my heart to become bitter. Jesus didn't pay the price that He did for us to be bitter Christians with unforgiving hearts. Bitterness is truly the root of all down-falls in our spiritual health. If someone can die from a broken heart, I truly believe a bitter heart can cause extreme problems with our spiritual, physical and mental health. It's part of what I call 'demonic distractions.'

> *"For our struggle is not against flesh and blood but against the rulers against the authorities against the powers of this dark world and against the spiritual forces of evil in the heavenly realms." Ephesians 6:12*

How many of us truly understand this scripture? I know I didn't! I knew that we deal with evil and people doing horrible things, but I thought the *people* were evil, thereby allowing the enemy to influence their behavior so much. I could never truly love people who repeatedly hurt me because I really had a hard time seeing them as a child of God.

During the Fast, I had one of the biggest breakthrough dreams ever. I had a dream I was on a bus when a giant tan scorpion came to fight me. It was the ultimate dual of a lifetime. We began wrestling and it seemed like it went on forever until I finally got it underneath me and crushed it under my feet!

When I woke, I asked Holy Spirit what my dream meant. But it took about a week of me searching Him out until I finally got the meaning of my dream: the enemy had been lying to me for a long time, but I was finally able to 'crush his lies under my feet'.

Once I got this revelation, people could no longer steal my joy! I can truly love, because I truly got the revelation that it's not people we are fighting against, it's *always* the enemy and his lying spirits. I see so many people venting about others on Facebook and social media, letting everyone steal their peace. They don't realize they are sacrificing their spiritual, emotional and mental peace to give more glory to the enemy.

Why let anyone have power over you? Love people and know that we are not those lying spirits. When we give in to the urge to blame, shame and accurse, we are literally giving the enemy an invitation to take some of our ground. I call it 'entertaining spirits' which came out of another dream I had where a bear came into my house. I began to feed him, give him attention and try to calm him down but when I turned my back, that bear began to tear up everything in my house! When I woke up, the Holy Spirit began to minister to me about 'entertaining spirits.' You can't make a wild bear become your friend just like you can't keep mingling with people that are not of the same spirit as you are. The more you give attention to people whom aren't walking with the Holy Spirit, the more you set yourself up to be a target.

Some people may say they are 'for you' but they are not really interested in your good. That's why we must "test the spirits." We are commanded to love, but sometimes loving from a distance is the best way to guard our hearts.

"Do not be misled. Bad company corrupts good character." 1 Corinthians 15:33

When you finally have had enough of having the wrong friends and you truly set your determination to be around people of good character, God will intricately place amazing people around you as you step out in faith.

I once heard a pastor say *'you can't fly with the eagles if you keep playing with the chickens.'* Another example Holy Spirit gave me about this was the story of the wineskins. I had a vision of people sitting in church and not even half of the church understood the message. That's when I realized an old wineskin cannot be filled with new wine. The revelations were flying over their heads due to their not having become new.

This is why fasting is so important. When we fast, we are forced to look at ourselves with eyes willing to see as God sees, and then we can begin to make changes, let go of what doesn't fit-in with our born-again, new-creation skins. There's always something to work on, there were things I realized about myself during the Fast that I think I could have gone the rest of my life believing the lie that *'I was fine.'*

God needs empty and willing vessels. A vessel is a container so if we want to carry the presence and power of God, we must first empty everything of the 'old creation' so we can walk out our new creation lives.

Pastor Megan Jordan often says, *"Fire falls on sacrifice."* I finally understood what that meant when the Fast broke me open. The most important (and most difficult) person we could ever need deliverance from is our own *old* self. I'll be the first to admit that my thoughts, attitudes, disobedience, and fears kept me from achieving or even seeing my destiny, and I couldn't take it anymore! I was willing to do whatever it took to become free, to become a vessel that God could use and raise up.

Say Goodbye to the Spirit of Fear

Holy Spirit spoke to me one day about the spirit of fear during the Fast so clearly: *"If you're a Christian and you've been saved for longer than ten years, but still deal with fear, you need deliverance."* I was like, *ok, I guess I need to deal with this thing.*

Nelson Schuman helped me so much in the area of deliverance. I have seen his ministry "Restored to Freedom" grow from its humble beginnings into him hosting a national television show. He has given his all to pursue the calling of God on his life.

Nelson helped me to become aware of the tactics of spiritual warfare. He helped me to identify the spirits which we deal with daily, and that I needed to empty myself of anything to do with the characteristics of those spirits, so I didn't interact with them anymore.

I'm extremely thankful for Nelson, and all the people God started to surround me with these past couple years when I made the decision to pursue God's dream for my life.

God wants us blessed and fruitful, but what good is all the wealth in this world if we don't have peace, or joy, or the fruits of the Spirit?

The joy and peace won't last if they aren't flowing out of our connection with God's Grace. I truly believe that's why we always feel like we want a bigger house, a better car, or a new this or that. The truth is that the spirit in us is starving for a real and truly intimate relationship with God! Our spirits are hungry for more of His presence, His Joy, His goodness. Nothing and I mean nothing can fill that void like the Holy Ghost. I would rather be poor on the streets with nothing than to be rich without the presence of God.

How to Avoid Trouble

I'll never forget this treasure I discovered during the Daniel Fast with Jesus. He lovingly gave me the best advice I had ever received in all my life. I had never heard this preached, I never saw it this way, I don't even ever remember hearing this scripture the way God gave it to me this day. God knows I hate conflict. He knows I don't like drama or trouble or mean people. So when I read this scripture, I felt like I Hit the lottery! Here it is. This is pure gold if you don't like trouble with people:

Proverbs 19, *"Those who respect the lord will live and be satisfied, unbothered by trouble."*

I said, *"What Lord? You mean I can live a life unbothered by people giving me trouble? Why didn't you give this to me years ago?! How Lord? How can I live a life unbothered by trouble?"*

His response was this: *"Respect My people and honor everyone in your life. Show them the utmost respect and love them the way I love you."*

It just really hit my spirit like a ton of bricks! So I said, *"How do I love them like you do?"* He said one word: *"SACRIFICE."*

That changed my life right then and there. My spirit got filled with revelations!

He said, *"You must make sacrifices to love the way I do, to lay down your life for a brother; to think of yourself last. The greatest among you is the servant. Repentance, true repentance, brings the clarity of the heart of The Father. With repentance, there's no excuses. There's no 'your side' is the right side."*

No wonder He says, "Love your enemies." We must have a foundation of love built underneath us so when every storm comes, we become stronger, not weaker. We learn to lean more on The Father than our circumstances. We must lean into the trials, not run from them. I spent half my life running and I was done. Hungry, unsatisfied, lost, broken, I cried out to God and He heard me, just as He hears all of His children. He always answers in such a loving way, but it does take practice, time, and diligence to hear Him.

"The fear and reverence of the Lord is the beginning of Wisdom."

In order to build a strong relationship as well as a strong character within us, we must come to God with respect and honor.

If you truly have a desire to hear the Lord and His will for you, you will do whatever it takes to get there. God will give you wisdom when you seek Him. If you want to know His dream for you, go on a journey with Him. Be willing to let Him empty everything out of you that doesn't bear fruit. Jealousy, envy, strife, unkindness, selfishness - if any or all of these are in you, Holy Spirit cannot rest upon you.

I could not believe I had any of these characteristics in me, but they were found there when I really let Holy Spirit work on my heart. They may have not been huge to me, but even the smallest amount needed to go in order for me to have complete freedom. I know that we can't reach perfection on this earth, but we can let His perfect love continue to work in us. It's all for His glory anyway. All you need is one second in His presence to be forever changed!

Birth Pains

Ministry is truly birthed out of having a love and heart for Jesus. It's birthed out of intimacy with the King. You can't birth something without a seed being planted and watered inside of you. It may not look perfect, in fact birth doesn't come without birth pains. It doesn't come without first carrying what God has placed inside of you. I was pacing and breathing uncontrollably when God started to birth all of this out of me. It almost felt like physically giving birth! It felt like I had no control of what was going on. All I knew was that God said, *"You have been pregnant for too long and you have to release this. You must also help and encourage others to release what they have been carrying as well."*

It is my mission to encourage and help others to reach the dreams that God has for them. The seeds are the Word of God that have been planted. Those seeds have been watered through hard times, blessed times, times of drought, and times of triumph. It's up to you to do something with those seeds. You can spread them all over the world if that's what you feel lead to do.

Chapter 3

Joseph, The Pit Is Your Platform

A Word for You

Acts 7:9 "Because the patriarchs were jealous of Joseph, they sold him as a slave into Egypt. But God was with him and rescued him from all his troubles. He gave Joseph wisdom and enabled him to gain the goodwill of Pharaoh, king of Egypt, so he made him ruler over all of Egypt and all his palace. Then a famine struck all Egypt and Canaan bringing great suffering."

My Sweet Child,

I love you with an everlasting love. It's My heart for you to love people the way I do.

The more you partake of Me, the more My love fills you.

I won't let you fall or go astray if you remain in Me and continue My teachings.

Everything that happens in your life becomes an opportunity for you to let Me work it out for your good. So, when the enemy rises up against you, when he brings people to hurt you, when everything comes crashing down around you, or you feel like you're in a pit all alone, know that I am with you.

I can turn any situation around.

I can give you great favor if you hold onto Me during the storms.

I don't waiver.

I don't change.

I always have a plan.

Even if all seems lost, I can find a way.

I can cause your enemies to be at peace with you.

I can reach into the furthest prison cells to wherever My child is.

Let your faith be built upon My Love, the solid Rock that stands.

I have rescued you before, I will do it again.

I want the best for you My child.

I will take you to new heights, you will soar, My child.

Take back your inheritance.

Have you ever felt like you were drowning, sinking in all of life's responsibilities, overwhelmed by all the chaos and drama of the world? Have you ever felt like you were alone and betrayed by every single person you have ever loved or cared about? I know I have. I know that I'm also not alone or we wouldn't have so many depressed people in this world.

One night while I still lived in Texas, I was driving and it was raining those big Texas-sized raindrops. The sky was lighting up with big bolts of lightning, and I guess since I was all alone - I thought it would be a great time to throw a great big huge fit to God.

I had been going through some major hard times of feeling alone and rejected by people I thought cared for me. I also felt like a single parent to four children because my husband had to work out of town for many years and I was not prepared for that or how alone I would feel.

Our son was always sick, and in and out of the hospital. Overwhelmed by sadness and torment, I cried out to God, *"Why are you having me go through all this Lord?"*

His response was amazing. There's only been a few times I have heard His audible voice and it's almost like electricity flowing through your entire being. I heard Him both inside my spirit and outside with my ears.

He said, *"Haven't I always made you strong through your sufferings?"*

All it took was that short simple phrase. I was awestruck by how He was so firm and yet also so loving towards me. When He speaks, it's like a thousand words in one.

When I have heard Him speak, I get visions and revelations all together. I saw flashbacks of difficult times which made me who I have become. I saw my childhood and how hard times made me a fighter. I was able to see how His strength was being made perfect in me. It's only been a handful of times I have heard Him speak audibly, but each time - it's been life changing.

He doesn't let us go through the valleys to leave us there. God is a gentle Father who sees so much potential in all of us. He roots for us, cheering us on just like we do for our own children.

> *"But He said to me, "My grace is sufficient for you, for My power is made perfect in weakness. Therefore, I will boast all the more gladly about my weaknesses, so Christ's power may rest on me." 2 Corinthians 12:9*

I can't tell you how many times people have turned on me, lied to and about me, and told me I 'would never amount to anything.' Too many to count. Now I thank God for it because they gave me a reason to prove them wrong, and those painful experiences made me stronger. I wouldn't wish the mental torment I have had to overcome on my worst enemy. At times, I just got tired of being judged.

Many times, I almost fell back into the habits of the past but God would not let me go no matter how many times I wanted to drink myself to sleep. Anything we spend the most time doing becomes more important than God. People want a miraculous encounter with God but don't want to give him ten minutes of their day. Relationships are built with a hungry heart. It comes from a place of wanting to know the other person.

Your Life Matters

When I reflect back on how many times I tried to take my life, or how many times I almost overdosed on crystal meth, I'm so thankful that I was able to overcome the attacks of the enemy on my life. When I realized he didn't want me here for a reason, I started to believe that God must have a great purpose for me. I will never forget that day my husband and I walked into our little home-town country church in Burney Falls, California.

Pastor Jerry Thomas was the senior pastor at that time. I had spent the last ten years as a strung-out meth addict, wanting to die every day because my life had no purpose or meaning. I had never experienced joy or happiness or a normal childhood like most of the people I saw in that church. *'How could they be so happy and joyful?'* I concluded, *'This has got to be fake'* until the pastor started to preach.

I remember when our eyes locked, it was like time stood still. I had never seen anyone illuminate such a powerful, beautiful presence of God. I could literally feel the tangible presence of God around him. I could see the love of Jesus on this man and in his eyes.

It only took that first sermon to break me and my husband. We were both instantly delivered from meth, two packs of cigarettes a day, alcohol, pornography, and many other things. Some things took a little more time, but we were both changed forever.

I had always known Jesus, and ever since I was little, I knew He protected me from the evil all around me. He was always with me, but I never knew Him like this. I was so tired of filling that empty hole with everything counterfeit of God. Everything else was just temporary and left me feeling drained and empty. I know what it's like to be so depressed you don't see what the point of living is. I know what it's like to be tormented in your mind, rejected, abandoned, and forgotten. I promise you, your life does have a purpose!

Let go of your past, leave it there and move forward, forgiving all who have hurt you. God will make something of your life.

You may have lost everything, you may be a mom who has lost her kids, a child who has come from a broken home, a pastor who is mentally tormented, a woman who's been forgotten by her family, a man who's been abused. You may be asking, *'what is hope? I have no hope.'*

Sometimes all it takes is one simple prayer of faith. If you don't have the faith or hope right now, that's ok. Try this prayer:

'Father, I ask that you give me the hope and faith to get through this. I ask that you give me the faith to believe you for great things.'

Surrounding yourself with positive people is so important! If you don't have a way to do that, pray God brings them to you, and He will.

Your time of being in the pit is over! This is the year for you to accomplish all the great things God has in store for you. Make no mistake, this life is short, we are here for a divine purpose.

"So go eat your food and enjoy it, drink your wine and be happy, because this is what God wants you to do." *Ecclesiastes 9:7*

This scripture tells me God *wants* me to be happy! He wants all of us to be happy! He didn't call us to be religiously bound, all wrapped up in trying to please everyone and live a perfect life. The best key to happiness I have found is continual fellowship with Jesus and letting Him work out everything in me. When I start worrying about everything else and everyone else, that's when I lose my focus and start to sink. On one of the days of the Fast, I started to lose focus. I started dwelling on things and anxiety started to creep in. I went to my room, got alone, put worship music on and fought against it with prayer. I then had a vision of me before the courts of heaven. I had my head down, I was crying and worrying. Jesus lifted my head with His hand. I looked into His eyes and He said, *"Only look here."*

I saw the galaxies and all of creation inside his eyes! Why do we worry or fear when The Creator of all the universe has us in His hands?

I've always heard stories of people having these miraculous encounters and wondered why some angel didn't beam down from heaven and tell me what my calling was. I realized each person that has experienced these encounters had experienced them out of true hunger for wanting to know Jesus.

"And without faith it is impossible to please God, because anyone who comes to Him must believe that He exists and that He rewards those who earnestly seek Him." Hebrews 11:16

You may feel like God is a distant fairy tale, but I can testify that if you truly go after Him, you will find Him. You're not going to know Him by going to church once a week and although that's good, it's not going to get you to the Father's heart.

Rise by Lifting

These last two years were extremely difficult for us. We made a big move with our family from Texas to California, then to Washington. I did not realize the affect it had on the children until my son came back from youth camp last summer. He opened up to us about how he was bullied all year long in school, even by a couple of teachers. He had thoughts of wanting to end his life, never knowing I had gone through the same thing as a child. This all came after a powerful prophetic word had been spoken over him.

I had no idea he was struggling like this! He seemed fine to me but would come home every day from school and sob in the bathroom. He took a razor to his arm and thought about ending it all. When I heard that, I about died! Our son Samuel had no friends in this new school that was in a bad neighborhood. What he did changed my life forever: he went to school and befriended a kid who was worse off than him. He started befriending the kids labeled as 'rejects'- the forgotten ones, the ones who didn't look like everyone else. He started bringing them to church and telling them about God!

He has since received paintings, letters and thank-you notes from several kids who said 'Samuel, I thank God for you.'

He started blessing his enemies, and he's now loved by so many! I love how he took a hopeless situation and made the best out of it. I know he's changed a couple kids' lives.

The enemy doesn't like people with strong callings. He always tries to make us feel like we don't belong. Considering that bad things are encouraged, our world has become so corrupt and if we don't make a stand, nothing will change.

I never told Samuel to do those things. I have just always tried to live my life by example. If you don't want your kids to do something, then don't do it. You're the best model they will ever have. It's your walk they watch, not your words. Sam's choice to make the best out of a horrible situation impacted so many people. The suffering he endured was turned around for Gods glory! It became a way for him to help others.

The pit can be the ground where our seeds are watered. The pit can be the molding clay that forms us for the palace. The pit can become a platform for us to help others and share our own testimonies. I am always trying to lift up others no matter what

I'm going through. It brings me joy to know even during my hard times, I can lift up another soul.

God is so faithful when I step out in faith, He is always there to lift me when I lift up others. Don't get stuck in the pit looking up and complaining to everyone about you being in the pit, or any situation. Instead, pound some steaks into the sides of those walls and start climbing! Get some of God's words into your heart and speak out His declarations until you start seeing those things come to pass! Eventually, you will start rising and when you make it to the top, nobody will ever be able to throw you back in.

Chapter 4

He Holds The Vision

A Word for You

Hebrews 4:8 "Draw near to God and he will draw near to you."

My Beloved Child,

Take rest in My love.

My love overcomes every hardship that raises up in your life.

I desire more of your attention, more of your fellowship. I'm hiding to be found, if you desire to know Me, you will.

I'm always faithful to meet you where you are.

I remove all your offenses like a cloud leaving the sky. I keep no record of your sins. You're forgiven.

If I forget the past, so should you.

Receive the gifts that I have given you.

Come away with Me, come sit with Me. Learn from Me.

Whatever you ask is yours.

There's great power in your words.

I will cause you to rise up above your enemies. I will strengthen you like David. He came to Me for strength, so I gave it to Him.

I will provide for your every need.

Get your fight back.

There are some days that come and hit us like a ton of bricks. One thing happening after the other. It all starts building up until someone explodes. Ever been there? I would love to add a laughing emoji right here.

I have worked extremely hard to get to a place of peace in my life so that when these instances occur, I'm not turning into a raging maniac! Nice and sweet at church, and a complete nut when all hell breaks loose at home.

Inner change does come, so be encouraged! It does take spending intimate time with Jesus as well as sacrifice. It takes making the decision to be a living sacrifice, knowing that God has called us out to be different for a reason. We're not supposed to look like the world, act like the world, or talk like the world. If we don't take the time to let Him work out all the wrinkles, we won't look any different than the average 'Jim Bob the alcoholic' who screams at his family every weekend, or 'Jan, the perfect lady next door' who mops her floors ten times a day, has a mouth like a sailor, flips out about every little thing going on in her life, and gossips about every friend she has. I don't want to be Jim Bob or Jan. I want to be the daughter God has created me to be.

I know that if I make a choice to go after Him, He will meet me there and He will meet you there too. I know there's been many times I felt distant from God. I thought it was because He was mad or angry at me but really, it was because I pushed Him aside to pursue my own selfish reasons. I stopped spending time with Him because I let circumstances of life get in my way. I let the waves overtake me. I allowed doubt to creep in and darken the light of His promises.

He gives us words of knowledge with prophecy and filled with amazing promises that we often expect to happen overnight. We try to make it happen like Abraham did instead of trusting His timing. I have caused myself a lot of unnecessary heartache that could have been avoided had I just let God deliver the dream He built in me.

The world is constantly pulling on us, saying *'oh you have to be like this person or you have to compromise to fit in and not be rejected anymore.'* So many lies of the enemy are being uncovered this year. Jesus did not compromise who He was to reach the lost. The lost came to Him because He stood out, He was different, unwavering, and solid. If we ask Him for something, He will not withhold it but everything is in His timing. He knows the right time as well as the best time. He cares about every single little detail so very much.

What Does It Look Like for Me?

You may be wondering what your life and ministry will look like. I can tell you that you may have some characteristics like some of your favorite people, but your ministry, destiny, or calling will be one of a kind. There are so many people I have looked up to in the faith and thought, *'I want to be like that person, and I want to walk in this gift or that gift.'* Jesus is so graceful and loving! He really does want us to be blessed and walk in all He has for us, but He wants us to figure out what it looks like for us. You will know in your heart and you will find these answers in your time alone with Jesus.

Be Careful What You Pray For

When I take a look back on some of my old devotions and declarations, I am almost ashamed at how selfish they were. I wanted all the things God could offer on this earth: wealth, a boat, a home. It was all about me. God may give us all these things, but none of it is worth having if we don't first pursue real joy, peace, and love in our own hearts and homes.

I wasn't declaring great things over my life, health, family, children, or the most important thing of all: my relationship with God. I can look back and see when my prayers were focused on me and what I wanted that I never had true happiness or peace. I only wanted God at that time for what He could do for me, or when I had something horrible happen.

If your prayers only go up to heaven when you have a crisis, you are in line for disaster! We should instead be in constant communication and fellowship with God.

To build relationship, it takes talking and listening, waiting on Him to answer and speak to us. How can we hear Him if we're always the one talking?

He doesn't respond to tantrums either, I have tried that a few times. The last time I did it, I had a vision of what I looked like standing before him throwing a fit before the throne of God. It was the most embarrassing thing I have ever witnessed! I never wanted to come into His presence again acting that way. He is moved by our Faith. "Faith can move mountains." (Matthew 17:20).

In or Out of Season

On about the fourth day of the Fast, I was busy cleaning around the house. I started thinking about what kind of 'season' this next year was going to bring, when I heard Holy Spirit say, *"This is an 'In or Out' season. People are either all the way in or out. Some are going to be left behind. This is the year I'm calling My children to possess everything I have for them."*

I was like '*WHAT?! I'm in Lord, I am in!!*' I understood that this year is going to be unlike any other year we have ever seen! Those whom are truly hungry will be used by Papa. Something that keeps coming to me is I believe we will see the greatest move of God we may have ever seen, with revivals and miracles, and signs and wonders following. Even that we will start seeing miracles on the news! I declare we will see more positive news with signs, miracles and wonders: limbs growing out, blind eyes opening!

Currently, the world system has control over what is put on the news. We are called out, a Holy nation of kings and priests to The Lord, and moving in the supernatural is our destiny and calling.

"Because you are lukewarm, neither hot nor cold, I am about to spit you out of My mouth." Revelation 3:16

Considering this scripture alongside the 'In and Out season' which Holy Spirit revealed to me, I decided, '*that's it! I'm going to do whatever it takes to pursue Jesus, my calling, my destiny, and God's heart for me. That's it, I'm done! I can't live my life with one foot in anymore. I'm going to give Him all I am.*'

Apparently, God would rather us be all the way in then half-way in. When you're half-way in, you look and act just like the world and you're distant from God's heart. To truly find Papa's heart, it requires sacrifice.

He didn't share this secret with me to scare me and get me into fear. I believe it was to excite me, to push me forward, to help me into the places where He is taking us, to see that He doesn't want us to miss it. He doesn't want any of us to miss out on this! It's truly going to be the most amazing outpouring the world has ever seen! He will use who He chooses, and He will use 'the hungry.'

During the Fast, Jesus started bringing the most amazing friends to me, people that just came out of nowhere to help lift me up, encourage me, and cheer me on. One of the most amazing friends I have ever had came into my life during the Fast.

She is going after God with all her heart, and has given up everything for Him. She is in a constant state of emptying herself to pursue more of God. She has gone through severe persecution, trials, and people just lashing out at her but she only shows them God's love. She also keeps me in line and is not afraid to speak truth to me if I start wavering.

We all need a friend like this, someone that can hold us accountable without judgement. I could easily see her hunger, and all the seeds she was sowing that are going to bring about a huge harvest blessing. I could feel she was going to start seeing angels in the supernatural, and she surely did. If you're hungry enough, you will experience the supernatural. If you're determined and don't quit, you will begin to see God work in your life.

Recently, I was sitting in my living room at around nine o clock, spending time with God and seeking Him, when the fire of God fell on me unexpectedly! I started trembling and felt like there was a swirling and increasing power inside, like a volcano about to erupt!

I felt God telling me, *"Release this."* But I wondered, *'how?'* then 'Facebook Live' came to my mind, so I jumped online!

I started flowing in 'words of knowledge' and giving testimonies of how God has moved. Many people were touched and healed! I have never seen myself as a speaker or a teacher or pastor, but when Papa told me to move, I knew I had to move!

I had so much stored up in me, I couldn't hold it in anymore! I had to share the goodness of God. I had to testify.

The enemy has tried to keep me quiet and choke me out of everything all my life, telling me *'nobody cares what you have to say.'* He will tell you what you went through was your fault, and your testimony doesn't matter. I have even had pastors tell me my testimony didn't matter because that's not who I was anymore!

When God has taken your life and made it completely new and changed who you are, your testimony could save someone else's life. There's so many hopeless people out there that need to hear more than *you can make it through* whether it's because of rape, molestation, all sorts of abuse, poverty, or addictions. People need to know there really is a loving God who can and wants to give us all a better way, and He comes in like a flood to make it happen.

The enemy surrounded me with pornography from an early age. I was even forced to watch it. When I asked God why that happened, He showed me that the enemy was trying to pervert my "vision" and that if the enemy can pervert our vision, he can steal our future. If he can keep us looking at every distraction and worldly opportunity, or create lusting desires, he can and will steal our God-given dreams.

You are giving him a way to create trouble and discord in your marriage by allowing lust to gain entry into your thoughts. It's not God who allows or does anything like that to punish anyone or 'teach them a lesson' as some have believed.

The only access the enemy has are from the unnoticed doors we leave open for him. There's many tricks the enemy uses to find or help create open doors into your life.

"Be alert and of sober mind. Your enemy the devil prowls around like a roaring lion, looking for someone to devour." 1 Peter 5:8

If he is always on the move looking for a weakness, we should always be one step ahead. We should not only "guard our hearts" as Proverbs 4:23 advises, but we must also guard our thoughts and emotions, choose wise friends, and also be aware how we spend our time.

If you're losing focus or stressed out, you may need to reevaluate your life. What can you perhaps decrease to bring peace into your day? What can you perhaps do more often to bring in joy and laughter?

"Set your mind on things above, not on earthly things." *Colossians 3:2*

If we can focus on the ways of God, and train ourselves to repeat those ways, then God really does manifest Himself in and through our lives!

How many times have you sat around day-dreaming, seeing vividly pictures of things happening around you. I honestly didn't realize I'd let more bad visions come into my mind than good. I let fearful images play out in my mind, picturing horrible accidents or what it would look like if this or that happened. God gave us an imagination, but not so we could envision the worst possible scenarios!

I truly never realized that the scriptures in the bible could change my life by changing my vision. One day during the Fast, a person in my prophecy group messaged me about seeing into the supernatural. He only gave me one scripture, Ephesians 2:6.

"And God raised us up with Christ and seated us with Him in the heavenly realms in Christ Jesus." *Ephesians 2:6*

It hit me like a ton of bricks! My teacher in LSGA (school of supernatural) was talking about "soaking time" with Jesus and how the more he placed his thoughts and affections on Christ, the more he would see into the supernatural realm and have experiences with Christ and His presence.

During one such episode, as I focused my thoughts on Jesus, I saw myself before the courts of heaven. I was very upset about a situation when Jesus put His hands under my chin, lifting my head and my gaze fixed upon His eyes.

When I looked into His eyes, I fell deeper with every second. I could see the galaxies inside His eyes, and all of creation stirring inside of Him!

He said, *"Daughter, only look here from now on."*

Jesus wants our vision to always be focused upon Him, because He's the center of the universe.

"For in Him all things were created: things in heaven and on earth, visible and invisible, whether thrones or powers or rulers or authorities; all things have been created through Him and for Him. He is before all things, and in Him all things hold together." Colossians 1:16-17

He wants us to base every vision, every dream, and every thought upon Him. He knows everything without us even having to tell Him. He already has a plan, He's just looking for people who are hungry that will focus their vision on Him, the One who makes all things new. He is looking for people that will not look to the left or to the right, but to hold focus on Him.

If you don't have a vision, ask God for His vision for you and ask Him to give you dreams. He won't leave you empty handed if you are truly seeking what He has for you. He wants us all to experience a breakthrough life but it all depends on us, and how far we're willing to go.

What are you willing to let go of to get to your created destiny?

Chapter 5

Cultivating the Dream

A Word for You

Zachariah 10:1 "Ask the Lord for rain in the springtime; it is the Lord who sends the thunderstorms. He gives showers of rain to all people, and plants of the field to everyone."

My Child,

Look around at this crumbling world. It saddens My heart that people who know My ways continue to walk away from Me.
It's better for those who don't know my truth.
There will be many who come into your life, all you need to do is love them by letting Me love through you.
Think good thoughts towards others. I don't put bad thoughts in your mind.
Some people you must love from a distance, but the key word is still Love.
I'm about to pour out abundant rain showers in your life.
My sweet child, I will keep you from evil. I will not let your feet slip off the path.
You will overcome them by My words, My truth.
You will be stronger and grow in strength and wisdom.
Be on alert always, for the enemy is always looking for an open door.
Rejoice and be glad always in everything.
The end result is worth the fight.
You are my joyful one. May you always keep laughing and be happy, it's a gift.

Continue to share it with others.

I lift burdens with laughter. I renew strength with joy.

Light your lamp and keep it burning. I'm taking you on a journey.

Receive all I have for you.

*T*oday is your day.

I can't tell you how many times I have wandered, strayed and fallen down but He was always right there waiting to pick me up.

His mercies are renewed each morning. He has been a refuge, a hiding place from my enemies and those who pursued me constantly. He has never turned away from me, even when I have turned away from Him. His arm has always been quick to save me in my desperate times of despair.

In cultivating a relationship with The King, He continues to work out every crooked path in my life. As I mentioned earlier, I have been given many prophetic words, dreams, visions, and confirmations of the dreams God had for me. It was not until I removed myself as the center of the dream that my dreams started to take off like a rocket, jet-engine fueled with the fire of God!

The center of every dream, vision or prophetic word should always bring your eyes back to Jesus and to Him being the center of it all. If He is not the center or the main focus, every dream will crumble.

The dream is not about us. The dream is about Him. When I first moved to a new state, Jesus was speaking to me in my dreams. I saw myself standing on a foundation, the foundation was shaking and crumbling beneath me. I was falling to the left, falling to the right.

I heard the Lord say, *"Build your foundation upon My word, so you can stand."* He is so amazing! He already paid the price for us. He has already become the foundation! He has already given us everything to access the kingdom, but it's up to us to activate it. It's up to us to cultivate His words in our lives so that when the world around us begins to crumble, we have Him and His word to shelter us and to use to fight for us.

Jesus is "The Word made flesh" (John 1:14), and the way we activate the living Word is by learning the word, spending time reading or listening to the word, and getting that word down in our hearts and spirits. Jesus used the scriptures when the enemy came to tempt Him in the desert. He spoke the words, "It is written." All He needed to do was be still and speak a word, a God word!

How many times have you gone through hard times with people or instances in life and forgot to speak the word of God over the situations? We start speaking our own words, things of the flesh, and that's when the world around us begins to crumble.

If you're having fleshly attitudes, your foundation is slipping, and before you know it you're falling right back into the traps the enemy set for you. Trust me, he's caused me to fall so many times, but I finally caught onto his tricks.

He pokes and pulls and irritates us through unsuspecting people, until finally it's enough and we end up lashing out. He comes to steal, kill, and destroy, and most of us are blindly giving him the power to do so. We leave doors open to his attacks by allowing bitterness and unforgiveness to take hold in our thoughts and feelings. You have to get to the place of saying, *'No person, no circumstance, no lie, will hinder my progress anymore!'*

Jesus payed too high of a price to have bitter roots growing deep in our lives. I'm reminded of a certain circumstance I went through years ago. I kept chasing after a "friend" I thought truly loved me, but this person just could not stop lashing out at me. They would always throw insults and put-downs without cause, and eventually I was walking around with my head down and hurting again. I started to become angry at this person and as I fell asleep at night, I felt the root of bitterness starting to form in my spirit. But the Lord actually let me feel what it felt like it, was horrible.

The closer you come to the Holy Spirit, the more you will be able to feel in the spirit. This was something I couldn't live with. It hindered every relationship I had. I was putting this person even before God without even realizing it. They had become the center of my attention. All the while they were going about their life, laughing, and enjoying life to the fullest, without a care that their harsh and condemning words had penetrated my soul.

I traveled around that same mountain many times before I realized this was about me. I was getting what I tolerated. They will have to give an account before God someday so why was I wasting so much time dwelling on what they were saying and doing?

Some people can really play the part too. The ones that bothered me the most were people that acted one way at church and another outside the church. To me, that's one of the worst behaviors a person could display. I grew up seeing many people do this in the church and that's why when I was given the opportunity to go to church many times, I said *heck no*. I believed the church was full of hypocrites and honestly, that's partly still true.

We are all a work in progress. I realized after God really touched my life that I had to do everything for Him, and not people. I had to find myself in Him for who He saw me as, not how others treated me. I thought the way people treated me was a reflection of how God saw me as well.

One of the biggest revelations you could ever receive is to view yourself as God views you, which is in a completely different manner than the world does. He looks at us through abundant love, compassion and care. He looks at us with purpose, destiny and joy! Whenever someone says something negative over you, God is always saying the opposite! They may say you're never going to amount to anything, but Papa sits in the heavens and laughs! He says *"You just watch and see what I do with My sons and daughters."*

When I first started recording music in Texas, a man that was managing me and helping me with all my music became angry one day after trying to take the credit for songs that I wrote. He called me on the phone and said to me, *"You will never amount to anything. You will never make it in the music industry."*

I paused for a minute and my response was, *"I will make it because I have something you don't – God, and He will make a way for me."* I hung up the phone, cut ties with him and two weeks later was contacted by talent scouts to go record in Nashville.

God's favor and love outweighs the thoughts, intentions, curses and hate the enemy has for us. When Jesus was being spit upon, whipped and lashed, and carrying His cross up to the mountain to be crucified, the enemy thought he had Him. He thought he had won when Jesus took his last breath, but really Jesus won it all!

So if others are against you, they are against God and God promises to deal with our enemies. We can't see the end result, but He does. It may look like your enemies are happy and winning right now but remember the enemy thought he was winning too. If you're on that side, I'm here to tell you - you picked the wrong side.

Jesus is coming soon. Time is running short for the enemy. It's not God's will for any to perish, but many will. We must pray for those who persecute us, for they know not what they do. *"Hurting people hurt people."* I know it's hard to always have to be the bigger person but remove yourself and let Papa be the bigger person for you. Let Him do it, He does it way better than we could ever imagine.

Watering the Seeds

When I begin to think about how many years I wasted on meaningless distractions, it almost makes me mad. I'm so thankful Papa has given me supernatural grace for my life!

It's never too late for anyone to live the life God has prepared for each of us. You deserve to be happy. You deserve to be loved, and to have people around you who believe in you. You shouldn't have to walk on eggshells around people, afraid of making them angry because you are a person who is allowed to have feelings. Holding back who you are because you're afraid of people getting mad at you for being yourself is not God's intention for any of us. What kind of life is that? Find people who love you and celebrate you for who you are.

I'm telling you, this was one of the greatest blessings in disguise in my life. God gave me the best, truest, on-fire-for-God people I could ever ask for! Even people who have their own successful ministries began to pour into me as I reached out. If anyone is too above you, or busy for you, that's not who God has for you. Don't feel rejected, just move on.

When I think about the great characters of the bible, two of my favorites are Joseph and David. They had to overcome so many private trials before the bigger ones came into play. Papa always shows me how they were watered before they sprouted.

David was a young sheep herder, a boy nobody ever thought would amount to anything, and eventually became the great and powerful favored King, raised up in the sight of all his enemies. He must have had big dreams as he spent countless hours out in the mountains tending to the sheep. I can just imagine how he would daydream of becoming a man someday to be used greatly by God.

He loved to worship and he watered his dreams by worshipping the Lord. He cultivated relationship with God the Father in his alone time. He had to kill a lion and a bear before he stood up to take out Goliath.

Papa has to build strength and character in us to prepare us for the greater. We can't just skip to the greater without overcoming smaller private trials in our lives.

Joseph, before he could become ruler over all of Egypt, had to endure his entire family betraying him, thrown in a pit to die, and was lied about and betrayed again. I look at what he did while in terrible conditions he didn't deserve and how he reacted through all the unfair tribulations.

As Christians, we are not going to escape the persecution. We are not going to escape the betrayals, we're not going to escape people lying about us but what matters is how we react to it all. Was Joseph going around telling his sob stories, blaming everyone for his problems, and wasting his time by constantly dwelling on what had been done to him? Was he looking to get advice or a prophetic word from every single person that he met? No. I know for a fact he wasn't. He would have never made it from the pit to prison, and finally - to the palace if he was doing what many modern Christians do.

We must get our minds out of and off the pit and onto the palace of all of God's promises for us. We all have a past, but we can't live there.

When I prophetically envision Joseph, Papa shows me how he watered during times of heartache, despair, and doubt. As Joseph was in the pit, I see him praying, seeking the Lord, praying for his enemies, and living by faith.

There's so much revelation in all the stories. There is so much more than the surface of the bible. As we grow in the Lord, we start to understand the same scriptures in new ways, it's amazing! There are *layers* to be discovered. There's innumerable lessons, and there's power in them for our lives today.

While Joseph was in prison, he was interpreting the dreams of others being thrown in the prison. He was lifting others up while he was in the most desolate place. The only way he could have known how to interpret dreams would have been by spending time with God, knowing who He is, and discovering His character.

He never gave up hope! His confidence was in the Lord, even though he was silenced for many years, forgotten, imprisoned, and lied about. He never gave up hope that God had better for him because he believed the dreams which God set in him. He refused to let his present circumstances make him bitter or fall into unbelief. He could have easily given up and said, *"There's no God. If there was a God, why would he allow all these horrible things to happen to me?"*

Instead, he spent all of that time watering and cultivating his faith, even when the darkness surrounded him. I can imagine how his body must have ached with pain, how his heart must have been shattered into a million pieces being separated from all he ever knew, his family turning on him, lying about him, and giving up on him, and being thrown out like a piece of trash. God was faithful to bless him in the sight of those who turned against him!

When everyone else sees us as worthless, an outcast, or trash, Papa sees us as a treasure. He loves to take us and make us new. He loves those people that are at the bottom and empty. It gives Him something to work with. How can He work with people who already have it all or are self-satisfied?

The only desire should be for Him. Then out of our desire for Him, He sprouts the dreams and He causes the flowers to bloom from the seeds we have watered in our despair.

Don't get stuck in the despair! That's how the process gets delayed. If you only watered a plant when you felt like it, would it grow? The same is with your life, dreams, and ministry. If you only water it when you feel happy or good, how will it be strong? How will it flourish? Gold can only be refined by going through a process. Don't despise the process!

"I'm here to get you to the next level," says Papa. Call on Him.

Silence the Religious Spirit

There was a time I lived in Texas for six and a half years. It was the most desolate, alone, and sad time I had ever gone through. My husband worked out of town all the time, while I was alone at home raising four children on my own. I remember thinking, *'I didn't sign up for this.'* I didn't get married to spend every birthday and anniversary alone. I did not sign up to be left doing every child's birthday myself, getting all the kids ready for church myself, and taking care of kids twenty-four-seven, without ever getting a break or any time to myself.

I had a few good friends, but the only ones that I was close to drained the small bit of energy that I had left. I have never been good at saying no. I gave of myself until I was completely empty and then would lash out at my husband when he would return home because I had no outlets or support. I was the one who always tried to remain strong while everything around me began crumbling. During this time, our oldest son was sick all the time.

I never got any rest or sleep for six and a half years. Our son had life threatening asthma, and chronic earaches to the point of almost complete hearing loss. He was in pain all the time, so much so that eventually he got used to the pain. He would scream and cry all the time. I couldn't take him anywhere because people would look at me like I was a horrible parent. Somehow, I still made it to church, but never felt better afterwards. I started seeking the Father in these times of severe persecution and depression.

When we moved to Texas, we were told that we were rebelling against God and that we were out of Gods will. These words affected me so much that I felt condemned, scared, tired, and weak.

So, I asked God for a word. Sometimes you just need to go to God for a word. I opened my bible right to the promises of Abraham! He said *"I have called you out. I will bless you and make you into a great nation."*

That's when I started to see how the spirit of religion tries to kill, steal, and destroy but the spirit of God wants to bless, uplift, and bring encouragement.

It's been over the course of sixteen years that I have begun to see that the religious spirit is always negative, always pointing out your flaws, and always trying to silence you.

God is always saying the opposite of anything negative coming at you. If the enemy can get you to come in agreement with what he's saying, he's got you.

I've had to distance myself from any and all people who were controlled by religious spirits so I could truly hear the voice of my Father.

Chapter 6

A New Name

A Word for You

Zephaniah 3:20 "At that time I will gather you, at that time I will give you honor and praise among all the peoples, among all the peoples of the earth when I restore your fortunes before your very eyes, says the Lord."

My Beloved,

I keep no record of your sins. I have forgiven you for all of them. The price was paid. Forget about the past. Leave it there.

If I don't remember your sins, you shouldn't either.

Whatever you ask is yours.

My sweet child, when I look at you, I see that you are beautiful and complete.

You're starting to walk into your blessings.

New days of triumph are on the way.

Stand tall and proud of who I have made you to be. You're different for a reason.

I have placed all the dreams in your heart for such a time as this.

All that has tried to stop you has only made you stronger.

You have prevailed in My love.

This is a time for the rains of My mercy.

I have made you like a light upon the hills, like a beacon proclaiming My words to the nations.

I'm a rewarder of those who diligently seek Me.

This is the year of dreams coming to pass.

There's nothing that you cannot do, there's not a thing that can stop you.

Your beauty outweighs the finest gold of the earth. I love to make beauty out of ashes.

I rejoice when you rejoice!

I have hand-picked you for such a time as this. I call you Mine My daughter.

My hand will not be held back from blessing you.

I couldn't wait for the day you found your calling and began to walk in it.

I will now lead you into the land where I have called you.

The day that I realized God wanted to give me a new name and make me a new creation was life changing for me. I had heard stories of God giving others a new name, and I thought, *'I have to try this.'*

During the Daniel Fast, I started seeking the Father. It was towards the end of the Fast when I was soaking, alone in my room with Jesus, that I started to see the heavens in the spirit.

I asked Jesus, *'Will You tell me what is my heavenly name?'*

And I saw it appear before me like a cloud, and in that mist the name *Anasha.*

I was filled with excitement! I had never heard this name before, so when my soaking experience was over I googled the name. To my utter shock, the name means 'powerful and complete'! The amazement at how much He loves His children left me shaking.

It was my hope to have a name I had never heard, and I had never heard Anasha! Still more astounding was that I was reading the course book from LSGA and it was describing how Jason Chin (the author) had also received a new name during *his* soaking time with God! His experience was pretty radical as well. It's likely I would have thought I was crazy had I not read Jason's experience immediately after the same happened to me. It just seemed so unreal, yet more real than anything I have ever experienced. I have never experienced the Holy Spirit confirming and showing me so many things in the spirit all at once as I did during the Fast.

I made it a point to really go after God more than I ever had. One of the things that really stood out to me was that I always wondered why I wasn't having any profound encounters, but never truly took the time to have any.

The soaking time has become one of my greatest addictions. It's so exciting to me every time Papa shows me something new!

There's so much that Papa has for us, but so many are not willing to take the time to really see what He has. It takes an emptying of all of our old selves so that He can dwell continuously in us. Holiness is still important to God. His word never changes. The more I saw how special and how important, and even how amazing I am to Papa, the more the cares of the world slipped away. I realized whoever is against me is against God, so why worry?

Get in the Mirror

There have been so many times I did not believe in myself. All I could believe were all the lies spoken against me. All I could see were my failures. I was so accustomed to closed doors and told no, being put on the back burner, relegated to the background. Rejection and abandonment, neglect and verbal abuse, slander and often forgotten had been the norm. People whom I trusted have told me that I would "never amount to anything." I've been the subject of gossip, been used, excluded, or made to feel like I didn't belong. When I realized Papa gave me a place to belong, at His right hand - everything began to shift in my life.

On one of my darkest, bleakest days, when there wasn't a soul to speak a good thing over me, I had enough. I realized that it was up to me to start speaking good things over myself and my life. I realized I needed to speak out-loud what Papa was saying over me, get it down in my spirit, and believe it. I knew what He was saying over me, but my mind and heart needed desperately to believe.

I went to the mirror and began to speak *'life'* - to speak purpose over myself. I let the truth start to sink in, and to intentionally renew my mind with the truth of God's word. I began to say things like *'I am called. I am anointed. I am special. I am favored. I am blessed. I am appointed. I am beautiful. I am amazing.'*

When the enemy tried to come at me again, his words could no longer penetrate into my soul. For every lie that had ever been spoken against me, I spoke the opposite which is God's Truth!

There's real power in our words, and with faith added to it, we become unstoppable! I'm not saying success happened over night, because there's a process. Some things happen quickly as a result of declaring God's words, and other deeply ingrained lies and issues take longer. The greatest thing about this is you're sowing seeds into your own life, seeds which Papa God will water.

As Romans 4:17 states, *"Faith is a substance."* We are to *"call those things which be not as though they are."*

Get in front of the mirror and start speaking out your rightful destiny! Start speaking those dreams and visions over your life as though they already are. If you don't believe it, say it until you do! Speak your healing until you see it manifest and encourage others to do the same. So many people are struggling with negatives and curses spoken over them, then watch how God encourages you.

Sacrifice

I love the story of Esther. She was a woman who lived in immense trust of the Father. She laid down her life every day, knowing that there may be others more qualified, more capable, and who had parents. Perhaps another would have appeared better-fitted to become queen. She had to continuously believe in who God said she was, when her heart said 'there's others more qualified'.

We all carry an Esther inside of us but it all really comes down to putting our trust and confidence in the Lord and allowing Him to flow through us. It's about His confidence, not ours. Without Him we can do nothing.

Esther had the revelation that her purpose was bigger than her suffering. What if she would have given up? We all play a big part in fulfilling God's plans. Esther laid down her life for a greater purpose than her own dreams. She realized her obedience required great sacrifice, and her great sacrifice would cause the whole nation to be delivered.

Her life up to that point was a preparation for 'such a time as this.' It was preparing her for her destiny. Even when she didn't understand, she kept moving forward, in faith and hope, towards the end goal.

Esther gathered all the Jews and had them hold a fast on her behalf, no food or drink for three days, in preparation for her to go before the king, which could have easily cost her life.

Perhaps she was so in love with Our Redeeming King that even her own life was trusted into His hands. It wasn't about her own dreams, or her glorification.

Papa made all her dreams come true. He gave her favor with all men because of her obedient love for Him. She left a mark in the world, not because of her beauty, or her talents or abilities, but by her sacrifice.

Our Lord Jesus left His mark in our World by His sacrifice. I often wonder what if He wouldn't have made it to the cross. What if He would have allowed every distraction, painful situation, or lie to offend Him? He focused instead on The Father, and the goal set before Him. His finished work at the cross now means that we can leave our mark on the fallen world, offering ourselves to be living sacrifices, allowing Jesus to live through us, in our place in the 'land' where He set us to intervene, just like Esther.

Jesus is the author of our story. He's looking for people who will trust Him to finish what He started. When you catch hold of this revelation, that our purpose is far greater than our own dreams, wishes, or desires - you will begin to function out of your true spiritual position in Christ. You will even look at others as *God's finished work*, as it states in 2 Cor. 5:16:

> *"Therefore, from now on, we regard no one according to the flesh. Even though we have known Christ according to the flesh, yet now we know Him thus no longer."*

They may not be where you think they should be, but that doesn't matter because when God looks at us, He sees the end result. You can wake up with joy each morning knowing God supplies all that we need to complete our destiny. He Himself is the main resource! The definition of resource: "supply, reserve, supply-store".

> *"My God will meet all your needs according to the riches of His glory in Christ Jesus." Philippians 4:19*

That tells me everything we need is found in Jesus Christ. He's our supply store! He owns the store house! He thought of us before we were born. He has great things for us.

Abraham's Dream

I love how God worked in and through Abraham. I bet Abraham really had a hard time trusting that his dream of having a blood heir could ever come true after reaching such an old age. He even sabotaged that dream by taking his own path and having a baby with another woman.

Abrahams dream was to birth a son, but God's dream was to birth a *nation*. God wants to birth a nation through us. His dreams and visions are always far bigger than our own. Even though Abraham messed things up, God was still faithful to His promise and turned it around.

It was when Abraham laid down his dream that God provided the ram (male sheep with its head caught in thorned branches). As soon as I laid down my dreams and humbled myself by trusting that God would bring it to pass in *His* timing, then God started to work. Suddenly, doors which had been closed, and those which I never knew existed, began to open and bless my life.

A humbled heart knows that trusting in God's ability and timing is the proper position to take. It's what pleases Him, for us to take the path of *faith*.

Humility

Humility is one of the major keys to unlocking the fire of God in your life. I remember when I first read Nelson Schuman's book, *"Keep Your Peace On"* - I didn't want to believe I had any of the symptoms he wrote about. People who have been wounded by either parent; or, who suffered sexual abuse; or had gone through *any* abuse, or were still held in the grip of an unresolved past.

If we don't deal with those issues properly, we leave an open door for the enemy to continue controlling our thoughts and emotions, which eventually lead to actions. The enemy works in the mind, whispering about our failures, and also the failures of other people. We develop "better than" attitudes, needing to feel better than others as a counter-attack against our shortcomings. This causes a sort of false pride, which if left to bloom into a character trait, turns us judgmental, mean-hearted, jealous, and critical. In many cases, unresolved wounds cause us to remain a victim of a person or situation.

These wounds steal our joy and peace, leaving us in constant strife. When I first read Nelson's book, I could think of many people who had such characteristics. He calls those characteristics as being the evidence of "spirits of Jezebel, Ahab and Leviathan." People who operate out of the spirit of Jezebel wind up being controlling, sexually demanding, and manipulative. Many times, I have seen people with this spirit have no remorse for how they treat others. I have always had this spirit lash out at me because of the prophetic calling on my life. Jezebel can imitate prophets, but she tries to destroy the true prophets of God.

People with this spirit manipulate others in the church into trusting them and thereby gaining positions of authority but behind pastors' backs, those people controlled by Jezebel are intentionally demeaning to those they should be serving.

They often have the Leviathan spirit as well, which is extremely prideful, acting as if the world 'revolves around them.' They will outright lie, or 'twist' the truth, causing unsuspecting innocent people to be seen as corrupt bad guys. They provoke suspicions and irritations to develop until the innocent victim blows up - completely unaware that they are dealing with a spirit. I fell into this trap so many times that I finally caught on that it was caused by tricks of the enemy. I have nothing but peace in my life now!

The Ahab spirit is very passive and usually gets controlled by these other two spirits. I personally related myself to the Ahab spirit's influence, as I've always allowed people with Jezebel and Leviathan to push me around and torment me. I unknowingly had many unresolved wounds from my past from various forms of abuse and even from being in relationships with people who had these spirits.

I renounced all of them and the key to getting rid of them is admitting to God you may have them, and ask Him to forgive you for the blindness. Then the explosion of God in my life was crazy! I started looking at myself, and I could clearly see others in my life who still operated in these spirits. As soon as I humbled myself, God started bringing the most amazing Godly people into my life, true friends, and people who truly love the Lord. I have done Nelson's prayers with my entire family. We are all now aware of the enemy's tricks and we steer clear of people who still allow these spirits to operate in their lives. Even though I didn't have severe symptoms, there were still things God showed me. I did not think I had a jealous bone in my body but He said, *"You know when you see people from the church hanging out and having fun? You have questioned why you were not invited."* I completely humbled myself and let God rid me of anything or everything that could keep me from moving forward.

As soon as I said that prayer, He surrounded me with the most amazing people I have ever met. Everyone says they want to be used by God, but not many want to let God clean their slate so that He can remake us. It's not your fault if you have been abused. That was an amazingly freeing revelation for me when I realized none of it was my fault, though I did have to take responsibility for my actions after being abused. I now have an anointing to see these issues on others to help them gain freedom.

False Humility

On one of the last days of the Fast, I asked Papa, *"What is false humility?"*

He said, *"False humility is when people act like they're happy for other people getting promoted or elevated, but really they are asking Me 'why hasn't that happened for me?'"*

That truly spoke directly to me! I have made it a point when I see someone getting blessed or promoted to now be sure to say, *'God, if you can do it for them, you can do it for me.'* I can testify that He has done everything for me which I have by faith believed. There are a great many people being raised up in the kingdom of God right now of whom have never been heard. God's been searching for people that have been hidden out in the fields, like David, for such a time as this. Everyone else around David was full of pride, believing they were more qualified, they had more knowledge, or they had better standing. God said, *"No, I want that humble boy who is after My own heart. I want that boy that nobody thinks matters. I want that boy that everyone has tried to shut up, keep quiet, and push around. He has My heart, he seeks me in the quiet places when nobody else is around or looking. That's the one I want."* Can you imagine the anger and outrage his brothers must have had? They couldn't believe that David was the chosen King! God loves to shock people. He loves the underdogs, the outcasts, the forgotten, those which the enemy has tried to keep silent.

During the writing of this book, I had a dream that the enemy had been trying to silence me by putting stones in my mouth. God opened my mouth, took the stones out, and put the stones in My hands and I started to throw them all over the world. There's been so much stored up in me! Now Papa is helping me to release all of it. I have stopped being afraid to speak and tell my story. I have started speaking out, proclaiming the truth, and I feel free to be who I am. Stepping out in faith is opening many doors.

Chapter 7

Miracle Worker

A Word for You

Proverbs 8:11 "For Wisdom is more precious than rubies, and nothing you desire can compare with her."

My child,

I love to see your sweet face look upon Me.
It brings Me joy to see you finding the hidden treasures in My kingdom.
I'm about to pour out blessings like never before.
The better days are ahead of you.
Continue in My righteousness, burying my teachings deep down in your heart.
These treasures no man can ever steal from you, no matter what happens.
I'm building a foundation of character in you.
This great reward you will keep with you for all eternity.
It's very special to Me to see how you let Me take all the pain and let Me create something beautiful.
You are My wonderful masterpiece, My clay, allowing Me to mold you with My own hands.
Your pure heart is a hidden jewel that I'm unveiling before many.
It's due season for a magnificent harvest.
My love has been imbedded deeply into your heart.
I will continue to enlarge your territory.
I'm showing up more than ever before.

Nonstop revival is happening.

Angels are in the midst of your praises!

Shout for joy! Rejoice and lift your eyes and hearts. I have opened the gates.

Even more than what you have asked for is going to happen.

All that has come against you I will put under your feet. I will bless those who bless you.

Like Job, many have mocked you and turned against you but you have remained faithful, always believing.

I work all out for your good.

I'm sending a latter rain that will flourish and restore your house.

My daughter, I love you.

I have experienced many miracles throughout my life. It doesn't make sense to me to hear of people who haven't! What's normal life for me may not seem normal to others, and through it all, God has taught me to live by faith.

Our lives had been changing so much since going to church and giving our lives to God. It was such a miraculous experience in church the way we got delivered from all of our addictions.

Back in 2012, my husband and I lived in a little mountain town with a small population of three thousand. We were one week away from getting married when he sent me down the hill to purchase our wedding rings from Harry Ritchie's down in Redding, California. I had asked him if I should I take my daughter, who was three years old at the time, and he said to instead take her to her grandma's, bring along one of our friends, so I took a mutual friend of ours down the mountain.

On the way back, the friend I had with me wanted to stop at his uncle's house, saying he had to get something, so we stopped and he went to get "his stuff." That "stuff" he picked up turned out to be a bag of weed, which he proceeded to smoke in my car. I didn't feel at all good about it, yet when he offered me a hit, I went to take it but I just couldn't do it. I couldn't inhale it all the way, I felt convicted after all we had gone through having been instantly delivered at church.

Suddenly, I realized I was almost driving off the mountain at a high speed. I jerked the wheel back but I overcorrected, still going pretty fast. The next thing I knew, we were rolling across the road. I could feel my body crunching into the cement with every successive roll. I felt my head hit the cement and my body crunching and crumbling beneath me. I knew it was the end.

In desperation, I cried out to God with each roll. It seemed as if it was in slow motion, as if my life were flashing before my eyes. All I could think about was my daughter and who was going to be there to raise and take care of her. I cried out to God one last time as we rolled again, *"God please save me!"*

That's when I woke up, staring at the smashed-in open windshield with dirt inches away from my face, and hanging upside down. I unbuckled my seatbelt and fell to the ground, crawling out the tiny smashed window which I could barely getting through. Standing up brought blood gushing from my head. I fell down as my body started going into shock. Everything started going black. I was holding open my eyes because I knew if I shut them, I was going to die. I cried out to God one last time, *"God, please save me!"*

Then everything went dark. I felt my body started to fade away and I knew it was the end. Right at that moment, a woman grabbed my arms and said, *"Would you like me to pray with you?"*

I could barely speak, but somehow got out the words, *"yes please."*

She started to pray for me as I felt the presence of God starting to flow through my body. A peace came over me, and I started to perceive light coming back to my vision. It was all blurry at first but cleared.

Before me was a beautiful woman, though I can't describe her age or what she looked like really, she was just beautiful. She left me to go pray over my friend, who I could hear screaming in pain on the ground. She prayed for him and there was silence.

Suddenly I heard a man's voice from behind me saying, "Don't move. You have been in a bad wreck. I called 911, they are on the way." He was holding my neck. I tried to look around him and asked him where the lady was. He said with a stern voice, "Do not move! Your neck could be broken. There's no lady here. I was the first one to the scene."

I argued with him and said, *"No! There was a woman here! She prayed with me! I can see now because of her!"*

As they were loading us in the ambulance, I remember trying to look for her car. My friend was asking about her as well.

You can call this a coincidence, or a hallucination, whatever you want, but I know what I saw. I will never forget her, and I know whomever that angel or woman was, she was sent by God Almighty.

That wasn't the first time. When I lived in Texas, I was in three different accidents, in all of which God supernaturally protected me and my children. One time, I was driving by myself when I looked in my rear-view mirror and saw a large truck coming straight for my driver's door. Right before that happened, God had prompted me to pray in the Holy Spirit.

The truck hit my door, I could feel the metal crush into my head and body. All I remember saying was 'this is it. I'm going to die.' But I felt a hand supernaturally push back the metal from my head and body. The entire drivers' side was crushed in, and I walked away without a scratch.

Another time, I had just recorded in Nashville and then flew back home to my parents' house in California where my children were. My husband had a job in Reno so the kids and I went to visit him.

On the way back to my parents' house, we were driving through the mountains and it started to snow making the roads icy-slick. We were going down a huge hill that had no guardrails on the side and we started to slide, the wheel jerking all around. I don't know how I kept it from spinning. I just started to pray in tongues, asking God for protection.

The kids started screaming and crying saying, *"We're going to die!"*

I said *"No we are not! - start praying!"* We all started praying, when I looked in my rear-view mirror, and saw a large

semi-truck very close behind us, also losing control in the snow! I saw the entire front end of his truck tipping over, sliding as the back end of his truck was swinging up behind him.
He was about to slide right into us. The kids looked back and started screaming again!

I said, "No! I call on the angels! I call on The Lord!" I was trying to hold still the wheel from spinning and keep the car strait because if I lose it we would go off the cliff or into the mountain.

It was all in slow motion. I could even see the fear on the truck drivers' face! He was scared for his life. It was as if God let me supernaturally zoom in on every detail.

As I kept praying, my body was dead still, gripping the wheel. I glanced in the rear-view mirror again, and saw the truck drivers entire back-end swing out in front of him and crash into the mountain. It was a horrific sight for sure! All we could do was pray for him and for us at the same time. We had barely escaped the truck slamming into us, or pushing us off the cliff!

We were all in shock, and the car started to slow down, like angels had come on each side to slow us down. We got to the bottom of the hill trying to breathe. I did not stop driving, and as the snow was getting deeper by the second, I just wanted to get us safely home.

God had once again saved me from death. I still, to this day, do not know what happened to the man or if he survived. But I believe God had me pray for him for a reason. I tried to look up accidents but never found anything.

During that same summer, after I recorded some music in Nashville, the enemy had it out for me again. He didn't want my voice to be heard.

We were invited by some friend's in Reno to attend an air show. This was a girl I had brought to the Lord and she had become a great friend. The weekend before the air show, my kids were all playing outside when I suddenly heard loud screams and crying. I ran out from the bathroom to discover my three-year-old, Trinity Faith, had broken her arm. The kids had been playing on a wagon which tipped over and Trinity had landed on her arm.

I was upset and crying for her, wondering, *'how could it happen to my sweet little innocent child?'* Maybe I had some hidden sin, or I had done something wrong... at that time, I didn't know yet how much God really loved me.

The doctor did x-rays and said it was very close to needing surgery to repair. I called my friends to let them know the baby broke her arm so we wouldn't be attending the air show. She said all her kids were sick and they couldn't go either.

A few days later, my friend messaged me saying that an air plane had crashed into the stands and people died. Our ticketed seats were exactly where the plane came down. God had spared all our lives!

We may never know why things happen, but I have learned not to question God. He always knows and has a bigger plan. I will never forget the feeling that came over me. Here I was upset about my baby being hurt when really God was protecting us from being killed! To say 'He works in mysterious ways' is an understatement.

Another Great Miracle

Shortly after my husband and I got saved, it seemed that every demon in hell tried to kill me. I was in that car accident a week before my wedding and a few months later we were attending church regularly.

God was really cleaning up our lives and started increasing our faith. My little brother got saved and people in my husband's family started getting saved as well after they saw the miracles we were experiencing. I started witnessing to people and dealing with great persecution, but I kept moving forward.

I started having the worst migraines and was put on migraine medication. I had not had a menstrual period in months, was gaining weight, and my breasts were lactating. I kept telling my husband I was pregnant but he kept telling me there was no way, as he had been told by doctors he would never have children. Eventually I had to get further testing. I remember I was taking "CNA" classes when my Doctor came and got me from the class, pulled me into a room and told me I had a brain tumor! Shocked and crying, I thought, *'I'll never make it through this one'*.

I remember saying, *'Great God! I turn my life around to serve you and now I'm going to die?'*

So I broke the news to my family and my husband. Everyone was so upset but my husband's sister, who had become a pastor, knew the word of God and told us that the word says go to the church, have the elders lay hands on you, and you will be healed. I thought, *'Let's go! I'm out of options, and I don't want to have brain surgery.'*

"Is anyone among you sick? Let them call the elders of the church to pray over them anoint them with oil in the name of the Lord." James 5:14

It also goes on to say, *"...and your sins will also be forgiven."* One of my family members also called us and told us the same scripture. My husband took me to the church and we told the pastor what was going on and he immediately called on the elders and prayer warriors of the church. After service on Sunday, many gathered around me and began to pray.

My body started shaking, and I became really hot and tears started streaming down my face. My head felt tingly, like a vacuum was suctioning out everything from me. I felt God removing many things from my body. I started to feel lighter and lighter with each prayer. Then in a moment, I knew I was healed. I even said to myself, *'I'm healed. I know I'm healed.'* I knew that as soon as I went to the bathroom, I would start my period. I went straight to the bathroom and after months of not having a period, started my cycle right then! I was absolutely amazed!

I have been praying over people ever since for healing and I have seen many miracles, including praying three people off life support! One of them had his entire family lined up to say goodbye. He had been thrown out of his car and into the air. The report was that he was brain-dead and comatose. The doctors said even if he comes out of the coma, he will be 'a vegetable' and he would never walk, talk or have a normal life, with only machines keeping him alive. I said to his mom, *"No he will live."* She didn't believe me.

They were planning to remove the respirator that day after all the family could get there to say goodbye. I gathered up some friends that were there, we got on our knees and we said a prayer: *"God, I ask you to heal my friend. I pray that he comes out of this and that he will be the same and that he will walk and talk again and be ok. He will live and not die."*

It was my turn to walk in to say goodbye, but I did not go in to say goodbye. As soon as I walked into the room, he started to move. He started trying to pull at the tubes.

I started screaming at the nurses, *"He's alive! He's trying to talk!"*

The nurse looked at me and said, *"No he's not."*

I yelled, *"Yes he is!"*

Finally, they came running over and started removing the tubes from his throat. He sat up and said *"Rock on Sharell."* I just started laughing!

Today he is married, has a son, and plays the guitar in a band. I will never forget that day and I remember it like it was yesterday. I have always lived by faith and couldn't understand why others didn't. I have always experienced answers to prayer and God supernaturally providing but I've also gone through extreme persecution and times of suffering as well.

We lost our home in Texas due to foreclosure. We have lost babies due to miscarriages, our fourth baby was a twin but the other baby didn't make it.

I have suffered from close loved ones lying about me. I have suffered being stabbed in the back by people that tell me I'm their 'best friend.' I choose not to focus on those things, and I don't dwell on all the hardships or the losses. I continue to move forward and trust and know that God has bigger plans for us. If I dwelled on those memories or places of pain, I would not be where I am today.

When our son Samuel was given 'sleepy juice' before his tonsillectomy, he sat up and waved to the air in the hallway. He still doesn't remember he waved and said, "Hi baby Joseph!" That was the baby we lost when I was around four months pregnant. God has allowed Samuel to see his brother a couple of different times but we know he's with God, and that we will see him again someday.

We all have a story, but what really counts is what we allow Father God to do with that story. You could save someone's life just by sharing your testimony. You could inspire one person to keep going just by sharing how you made it out.

We may sometimes feel as if God's punishing us or mad at us but that's not the case. Whenever He closes a door, I have always said, *"He must have a better one."* Sure enough, He has always provided a bigger and better opportunity behind another door.

God wants to use you. He wants you to know Him and the love He has for you. I refuse to let the religious spirit keep me quiet anymore! I do have a story! I do have a voice, and it matters! My story does matter. It matters to God and He says, *"For whoever is not against us is for us." Mark 9:40*

Chapter 8

You're Free to Be You

A Word for You

Isiah 41:18 "I will open rivers in high places and fountains in the midst of valleys. I will turn the desert into pools of water and the parched ground into springs."

My Child,

I'm breaking off every chain, every fear of man. There is no need to worry what anyone is thinking of you.

What matters is what I think.

I have anointed you.

I go before you, removing every mountain in your way.

I will bless everything you do.

I will show them how much I favor and love you.

They may have disqualified you, counted you out, treated you unfairly, but this is the time I turn it all around.

They may have tried to silence you, shut you up and make you feel that what you had to say did not matter. But remember, 'whoever is last shall be first.'

The kingdom of heaven is increasing upon the earth.

You will be heard. You are a favored queen such as Esther.

You have approached Me boldly with a pure heart, therefore I will move upon your life.

My Child, get ready. All are about to see how mighty I am.

I send the command, I stamp you with my approval.

I bless whom I choose. I promote whom I have hand-picked.

Keep pushing forward. Think of every obstacle as a stepping stone: with each step, you get closer to the promise.

Although you have never seen yourself as being much, you have always been much to Me.

I will deal with those who have hurt you, as you continue to walk in love.

If you're always motivated by love, you will never lose.

This season has been one of the most freeing experiences I have had, finally truly broke free from the fear of man, and the religious spirit!

The religious spirit has kept me silent for way too many years. I would never speak up, always letting everyone talk over me and allow them to cause me to feel unimportant. I had to distance myself from every single person that made me feel this way, but God was faithful to bring people to me who accept me and love me for who I am.

When I started stepping out in faith, leaders in the church shut me down. I was crushed! The enemy was using them to cause me to think there was something wrong with me. As I said in the previous chapters, I just wanted to be accepted by everyone so much I wouldn't use discernment or wisdom and wound up surrounding myself with people who made me feel worthless. Finally, enough became enough.

Thankfully, Papa brought some very gifted prophetic people and mentors into my life who've helped me. If not for His intervention, I would have remained timid and closed down in fear. When I broke away this last time, it was one of the most freeing moments of my life. Where the Spirit of the Lord is, there is freedom!

I truly believe that children who are gifted, anointed and "have a calling" are being raised up this year. This is the year of "the underdog!" People who have been silenced, scared, and mistreated are being launched into ministry and destiny. I have recently watched a few people rise from the ground up in a matter of months.

There's a spirit of blinding pride in many western churches, and many pastors abusing their positions of leadership. We have started to see a great exposure taking place in many different states. People are leaving churches they have attended for years, dissatisfied with the religious 'routine.'

It has been difficult to find truth-seeking churches which operate in the gifts of Holy Spirit and inviting Him to disrupt the scheduled plan. The bible says, "Don't quench the Holy Spirit."

Just this year, I felt horribly sad to leave my church because I had made so many great friends but it was just not where God wanted us. I asked God for confirmation. I turned to the story of Moses and how they followed the cloud and I heard Papa say, *"You want to be where My glory is"* so I encourage you to be where the glory is. A gospel without power is meaningless, and I have to be where the power of God is manifesting.

My Best Friend

Can you guess who my best friend is? It's the Holy Spirit. Without His leading, I would not have become the person I am today. The more you get to know Holy Spirit, the more you will hear from Him. The more you grow in relationship with Him, the more He will guide you.

Praying in the Spirit is one of the most important things you could ever do. It's one of the best gifts from the Father because as you pray in the spirit, you're praying forth your destiny, and you're praying forth God's intended will for your future. You're speaking in your Heavenly language, which only God and your own spirit understand and it confuses the enemy!

The more involved I have become in Love Says Go Academy, the more I have been hearing Holy Spirit. A few weeks ago, I was at the gym and an older man next to me started laughing because he accidently changed my channel. I started laughing too, and he said, *"You're awesome."*

I pointed up and said, *"No, He's awesome!"* Immediately, I heard Holy Spirit say, *"He has three kids: two boys, one girl."*

I was just as surprised as that man when I further heard and said his daughter's name is *"Marie."* It was the first time I had ever gotten a name and it blessed him greatly to hear how much Papa loves him and how good of a dad he is to his children.

The more I have stepped out and relied on Holy Spirit, the more I have been able to hear in my spirit. Growth in walking in the supernatural or spiritual comes by desiring to know God and to give His love, and further by listening for Holy Spirit's directions. It's also by being willing to experience the mistakes which come from the "learning curve" of life. Those mistakes are a normal part of learning everything else which are also in the spiritual walk. It's okay, keep moving forward. The more you realize the gifts of Holy Spirit aren't about you and your abilities, but are from God, the more He can use you.

Walking in Love

"If I have the gift of prophecy and can fathom all mysteries and all knowledge, and if I have a faith that can move mountains, but do not have love, I am nothing." 1 *Corinthians 13:12*

"We will know them by their fruit" - right? I think we all know people who appear to be Godly. They seem to have it all together, know the scriptures front and side-ways, but there's no love being expressed in word or deed. We must be careful not to fall into that category, but we also must be aware of people like this in the church. The spirit they operate from is not the Holy Spirit.

They may be able to prophecy, preach, and pray for the sick and even see people healed. Behind closed doors, however, they are demanding, controlling, and competitive. These are who the bible calls 'wolves in sheep's clothing.' One day, they will stand before God and He will say, *"Away from Me! I never knew you."*

Look at the fruit of people who constantly take stabs at you or others behind their backs, when they start to feel comfortable around you. They appear to be righteous and so close to God in front of everyone else.

Some people act like know it all's, like they are more spiritual than you and only they can hear from God. These people are being manipulated by the Jezebel and Leviathan spirits. I have seen this in Christians more than non-believers. They are unaware of how much they are being used by the enemy, and they are extremely dangerous for your walk with God if you don't put your trust and worth in God alone.

As Nelson Schuman says in his book, "Restored to Freedom": *"Limit your exposure to people who strive."* It's not easy sometimes, especially if it's a family member, but we need to learn that no one is anointed to become a punching bag. We need to love them from afar instead of continuing to be entangled in their controlling schemes.

We must use spiritual discernment and keep our hearts free of offense. If we allow ourselves to fall into offense, we can quickly become bitter and we are blocking our own blessings. A root of bitterness can be extremely difficult to find and pull up.

Forgiveness is an essential part of following our Lord, and without a constantly close walk with the Holy Spirit helper, we can become entangled in the abundant opportunities to become offended. This leads to closing ourselves off from being used if we allow our hearts to turn inward by offense and not toward our calling: love and forgiveness.

Chapter 9

Your Legacy is How You Loved

A Word for You

John 10:11-18 "I am the good Shepard. The good Shepard lays down his life for his sheep."

My beloved Child,

You are on the path that I have called you to walk.

Sometimes you may feel weak or weary, but it's in those times that My strength is being perfected.

Don't let worry or stress weigh you down, continue to abide under My wings.

Trust Me My child, you are under My protection.

I won't let anyone harm you.

The attacks of the enemy may come, but I will rescue you.

I'm planting you on solid ground. This ground cannot be moved or shaken.

You will flourish in the desert, you will bear fruit in the dry lands.

Through the heat, storms, or droughts, you will stand tall.

I will bring refreshment. I will bring You provision. I will lift you above the dry and barren lands.

I loose the riches of My kingdom over you.

I'm stretching forth My hand, causing a great shift in the earth.

Times of change are coming.

The tables are turning in your favor.

I order all of your steps.

I'm always moving, even when you cannot see.

I will sustain you with My promises.

Pray for those who persecute you.

Keep your heart guarded. Envy, jealousy, and strife are not from me.

Your spiritual eyes are being opened on a greater level.

You are taking flight. My power is with you.

You asked Me for wisdom, so I gave it to you. I will not let you fall or be ashamed but I will shame your enemies and those who come against you.

I want to dedicate this Chapter to my step-Dad, Stan Glover, who passed away while I was writing the fourth chapter of this book.

Let me tell you about the man who changed my life. I thought I changed his, but really it was him who changed mine.

He raised me as His own since I was four years old and always encouraged me, even when he was in bad health. He was so excited for me to finish this book. I had planned on writing about him because of what an amazing man he was and I couldn't wait for him to read it.

It wasn't until the last year of his life that he started attending church. All my years growing up, I observed people in the church and never understood why they acted one way in the church and one way at home. I had family members who attended church while they were porn addicts at home, had severe anger outbursts, or verbally abused me. I was even left in a car in the summer heat with no food or water for hours at a time.

Childhood injuries also caused my step-dad to occasionally struggle with angry outbursts. His own childhood was filled with abuse, and he never got healing from being beaten with an extension cord at five years old by his own father.

He wasn't perfect, but for the most part, he was more like Jesus than any Christian I had ever met.

The way he loved people was remarkable, the way he forgave people was unlike any other person I had ever seen. He was always giving, always helping people out of a bind.

He gave everyone in his family a job. He was the most unselfish person I had ever known. He did everything for my brother and me, and he worked hard every day to take care of us. He always protected me and gave me good advice. He tried to teach me how to drive and even when I almost put him through the windshield going down the driveway, he only laughed.

I will never forget one night I woke up terrified because I had seen a dark shadow in my doorway. I screamed for his help and he came to my room and fell asleep at the foot of my bed. I always felt safe with him. I knew nobody would ever harm me as long as he was there.

Whenever I needed him, he was always there. He would drop everything to come to my side no matter what. Even when I became a drug addict and treated my parents horribly, they never closed their doors to me. They always welcomed me back in with open arms, never kicked me out, or told me I wasn't welcome.

I saw him go through severe persecution. He was slandered, taken advantage of, and hurt by people who claimed they loved him, yet he always forgave and always kept on loving.

Not one of us are perfect, we all make mistakes, but this man was solid even though he'd been angry with me a few times because I was an out of control teenager on drugs. He still didn't change or waver from who he was.

He always gave to anyone who asked without hesitation. I knew I could never preach to him after I got saved because he had been through the same things as I had. He grew up looking for God in every church but in every single church, he saw horrible things. He believed all Christians were hypocrites. He would clean up the church grounds after hours and see the pastors through the windows smoking and partying and messing around with other women after everyone left. He observed so much that he decided he didn't want a part of anything like that. I have more respect for people who would rather not claim to be Christians than to be a fake one.

He left a huge legacy to all of his children and grandchildren, all who are amazing and wonderful people. The way he lived spoke of who he was. He never had to prove himself to anyone. He was a man of integrity, character, and his word meant everything. He never made promises he couldn't keep or treated people harshly. He was always going out of his way to bless and help others. He lived his life in service and in sacrifice.

After ten years of him watching mine and my husband's life, he started to open up to God. It would bring tears to my eyes when he would say things like, "Only God could do this Sharell." His life spoke measures of the kind of heart he had. He was a coach for many years and all the kids he coached still called him Dad or Coach. So many people looked up to him and felt like he was more their father than their own.

When I truly take a look at his life, he was so much like Jesus. Everything he did was motivated by love. Jesus lived His life as a sacrifice, giving in everything He did, and was motivated by love.

I remember the text like it was yesterday, "Poppa fell in the bathroom and was unresponsive."

My heart seemed to break in half and I started to panic, but knew I had to be strong for my Mom.

I went and woke up my husband. We got all the kids in the car and drove all night long until we reached the hospital the next day in California.

I was believing for a miracle. He had survived an earlier stroke and two major heart attacks and had already lived ten years beyond what doctors had predicted.

A year before, Mom and Pop had called me and told me that he had congestive heart failure, and I prayed and said, *"No you don't have that Poppa! You're going to go to the doctors and they are going to say 'I don't know who told you that but they made a mistake.'* and sure enough, that's exactly what happened.

We had seen many miracles, so I refused to believe that this was the end. Pop had to be around for a lot longer.

But about a week before that, I got bad chest pains and had a nightmare of my Poppa crying. I woke up immediately and called my parents. I knew something wasn't right.

My Poppa had always been the strongest man I had ever known. He only cried a handful of times. Once was when I sang a song to him about what an amazing Dad he was. He was the toughest man I ever knew, so thinking of him being in pain or distress really upset me.

I called and of course he said my Mom was having chest pains, not him. Even when he was in his greatest pains and struggles, he always put others first. He didn't want us to know how much he was suffering.

On the drive down, I had a vision of him in Heaven looking back at me with the most beautiful smile I had ever seen. I called the hospital and my Mom put the phone up to his ear and I started commanding him to come back, even though I knew he didn't want to. I didn't want to lose my best friend, I couldn't lose my Dad!

Then my husband turned to me with tears filling his eyes. I hadn't said anything to him about my vision and he said, *"Sharell, I saw Whopper standing on the edge of Heaven. Jesus was holding his hand. He had a huge smile on his face and he was so happy."*

We both started bawling. Whopper was always a Dad to my husband (we all called him Whopper). He was his biggest support. He was his shoulder, his advisor and his helper. My husband never had anyone support him and give him confidence like my Pop.

115

Then our son, Samuel, woke up and gasped saying, *"Mom I saw Whopper's spirit! He was smiling at me."*

My chest was aching. I was starting to lose it. Then we got the call that the doctors said he wasn't going to make it, and my world shattered. It was like I was crushed. A part of me had died. Even though my spirit was telling me it was his time and he was happy.

It was one of the hardest things I would ever have to accept. Even my step-sister called and said, "Sharell, I feel like he's already gone."

I couldn't believe it. This was so sudden, you can never be prepared for something like this.

Then the enemy started tormenting my mind saying, *'if you're so close to God, why don't you pray him back?'*

When I got to the hospital, my heart broke in half. My Poppa was on life support, in a coma, with a severe brain bleed. I wanted to pray him back but I knew it would be selfish. He was happy and he was tired of suffering. It was almost like I could hear him saying, *'don't you dare.'*

I lost all composure, screaming and crying over him when I got my alone time with him.

I was not ready for this Whopper.
I promise I'll take care of Mom.
You were the best Dad I ever had.
I love you so much.

I can't even see through the tears as I write this. He was everything to me. He would always do this thing where he would roll my fingers through his hands when we would sit and watch family movies.

At the end, I held his hand thinking, *'This can't be the last time. I can't live without you! Who's going to tell me stories? Who can I run to? Who can I go to when I need a helping hand or I'm going through a hard time?'* Yes I have Jesus, but God knows how much we love our earthly fathers.

I started to sing the song for him that made him cry years ago, and a tear fell from his eye. They said he couldn't hear anything, but I know his spirit heard me.

I promised him I would take care of Mom, and I held him and hugged him and loved on him. I took as long as I could, even though people in the family couldn't stand to see him being kept alive like that. To me, he was still there.

My mom and I told him it was okay, that he could go be with Jesus now. I held him until he took his last breath.

It brought my heart so much comfort and joy to know that he had found Jesus and he had such a love for Jesus. Mom says it's because of how he saw God transform our lives, but I believe he always knew Jesus. He just didn't want to be a phony person.

At one point when I was crying and the grief was unbearable, I heard him say, *"Oh, quit squabbling over me, I'll be fine,"* which was one of the last things he said to me when he was still alive.

I wish I would have gone to see him sooner, but wasn't able. He wanted me to continue doing the things I was working on even though he had gotten bad reports from the doctor. We never thought he would have gone so soon after.

Poppa was best at loving people. I truly believe that's the best legacy a person can ever leave. He cared more about investing in people than in his own wealth or future.

Life is but a whisper. Yes, God wants us to be blessed, but what good are the blessings without love? You can't take wealth or titles or talents to heaven.

You may be wasting precious time here on earth, investing more in your physical gains then what God has truly called you to become. I encourage others to really seek God on their specific purpose. My Poppa would tell me how important my words were, and he even started to change what he spoke over his life after he saw God do so many miracles for all of us.

My Poppa had an impact on so many lives. He truly set the example for me that the biggest legacy you could ever leave here is how you love people. Everything you do has a profound impact on others. You may not see it today, but someday you will see how you left your mark.

We must build for the eternal future. After my Poppa passed, I took my Mom home to her home and then went to Dollar General, my Pops favorite store. They lived up in the mountains, so when the Dollar General came there, he was thrilled. I took our three-year-old daughter Taylyn. She didn't know Poppa had passed and we didn't tell her. She thought he was still in the hospital and seeing him there really upset her. He was her biggest buddy on the planet. She used to lay up on his belly as they laughed and played.

We left the store, and as I put her in the back seat, she gasped and said, *"Mommy, Mommy! I saw angel Whopper and he spoke to me!"* She said in these exact words: *"Remember, if I'm not around anymore, always remember to love people."*

I burst into tears! I was beside myself at how she saw this and know she saw him in the spirit! His last message was, *"always remember to love people"*.

In this life, we are all going to face great trials and tribulations, but God's heart is always restoration. We may have people do the most horrible things to us, but when they truly come and humble themselves, it's up to us to forgive them. Doesn't mean you have to be someone's best friend or hang around them and some things take time, but we all deserve forgiveness. Jesus made it possible for all of us to be forgiven. He paid the price.

I declare that if you have never felt the love of the Father, that today be the day you begin to see your worth. I pray you feel His touch, that you're able to let go of the past and the things that hurt you and let God make something beautiful out of it. If you trust Him, He will never fail you.

I can remember one of the hardest trials I went through in my life was when a close family member was severely persecuting me. This wasn't just persecution, they were literally trying to destroy my life but I clearly heard the voice of God say, *"If you are always motivated by love, you will never lose."*

That's when I truly let go and forgave. It doesn't matter how many have tried to persecute and slander me. I still love them. I know that God is a just God, and He will handle every battle for me.

Eventually, the truth prevails. As for me, God made too big of a sacrifice for me to be stuck in bitterness and unforgiveness.

The 'craziest' thing about going through trials is they bring about spiritual growth and maturity, and true closeness with Father God. I found that leaning into Him during trials and persecution have been the most amazing times of hearing His voice and knowing His love for me. I could not be who I am today without the love of God. He's completely taken a drug addict who couldn't read a book into someone who could write one. He took a broken, fearful, hate-filled, selfish person, and made me into a beautiful masterpiece. *God calls me His masterpiece!*

My final prayer is that if you have ever been sexually, mentally, physically, or emotionally abused, that you take those pains and everything you have gone through and let God write your story. Let Him make something out of it.

I bless and love everyone who reads this book.
Thank you for listening to my story.

Below are some life-changing declarations for anyone who wishes to read them and see your life change forever. God-breathed declarations and decrees are for you to take personally, for yourself. Say them with all your heart and soul, say them until you see them come to pass.

I declare my destiny is being birthed. My calling is coming forth. My heart is aligned with God's heart. I walk in purity and righteousness. My eyes only look to the Fathers and look upon good things. I will not look to the past, but I will look forward to my future, which will be amazing, because my trust is in God.

"You will also decree a thing, and it will be established for you, and light will shine on your ways." Job 22:28

Another translation says, *"You will succeed in whatever you choose to do, and light will shine on the road ahead of you."*

"For the wicked shall be cut off, but those who wait for the Lord shall possess the land." Psalms 37:9

I declare that I will possess the land God has for me.

I declare and decree light will shine on the road ahead of me in everything I do.

I declare and decree I will obtain all the Father has for me, I will walk in authority, grace, and power.

I declare nothing will keep me from my purpose, my destiny, and my calling.

I declare every door opens on my behalf. I declare everywhere I go I have favor with God and man.

I declare God will be glorified in my life and everything I do.

I declare God's dreams for me are coming to pass.

I declare angels are sent out on my behalf.

I declare God moves every mountain that stands in my way.

I declare I am blameless, and my heritage will be forever. I will never be put to shame. In the days of famine, I will have abundance. *(Psalms 37:18-19)*

I declare that I consider the poor and the weak, so God will always consider me. Blessings will always be mine. *(Psalm 41)*

I declare I have a never-ending supply. The wicked borrow but my supply never runs out. *(Psalms 37:21)*

I declare the Lord sits in the heavens and laughs at my enemies.

I declare the wicked fall into the trap they set for me.

I declare my enemies come to know the Love of God.

I declare my enemies vanish like smoke, and when I look for them, they are gone.

I declare I love people as Jesus loves.

I declare my heart grows closer to God every day.

I declare and decree I do hear God's voice.

I am anointed to preach the gospel, heal the sick, raise the dead, and cast out demons.

I am anointed to set the captives free. The one who is freed by the Son of God is free indeed.

The Joy of The Lord is my strength and I am full of the joy of The Lord! Depression, anxiety, and fear have no place in me! My heart beats to the rhythm of God's Spirit.

I declare I am strong and full of abundant Life!

By Jesus' wounds I am healed!

I declare God takes my misfortunes and make them His story. I will leave a legacy.

The Kingdom of God manifests through me, and I am a world changer!

I declare God's face shines upon me and I am blessed when I go in and when I go out.

I declare no word or curse spoken against me will ever come to pass.

I declare no weapon formed against me will prosper, and every word spoken against me will be shown to be wrong!

God's abundant grace and wisdom go with me and abound in those around me.

God Himself is the lifter of my head!

I humble myself before The Lord, and He vindicates and honors me.

I am blessed and highly favored of The Lord. I am accepted in The Beloved!

Fear of man is broken off of my life and I am victorious!

References

The New International Version Bible

The New King James Version of the Bible

The Message Version of the Bible

The King James Version of the Bible

The Parallel Bible with four different translations

Notes

Notes

Notes

Notes

Notes

Notes

Made in the USA
Lexington, KY
20 May 2018